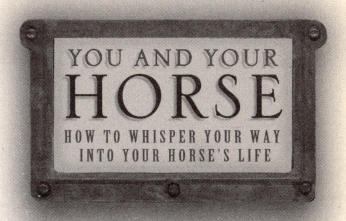

YOU AND YOUR
HORSE
HOW TO WHISPER YOUR WAY
INTO YOUR HORSE'S LIFE

BY DANDI DALEY MACKALL

ILLUSTRATED BY
JEFF O'CONNOR

ALADDIN PAPERBACKS
NEW YORK   LONDON   TORONTO   SYDNEY

I DEDICATE THIS BOOK TO ALL OF MY HORSE-
LOVING READERS. YOU KNOW WHO YOU ARE!

 ALADDIN PAPERBACKS

An imprint of Simon & Schuster Children's Publishing Division

1230 Avenue of the Americas, New York, NY 10020

Text copyright © 2009 by Dandi Daley Mackall

Illustrations copyright © 2009 by Jeff O'Connor

All rights reserved, including the right of reproduction in whole or in part in any form.

ALADDIN PAPERBACKS and related logo are registered trademarks of Simon & Schuster, Inc.

Designed by Lisa Vega

The text of this book was set in Century 731 BT.

Manufactured in the United States of America

First Aladdin Paperbacks edition January 2009

10 9 8 7 6 5 4 3 2 1

Library of Congress Control Number 2008926925

ISBN-13: 978-1-4169-6449-0

ISBN-10: 1-4169-6449-5

CONTENTS

INTRODUCTION

Anyone who's watched a magnificent horse gallop across a pasture can't help being moved by the beauty and power of horses.

Some of us, though, don't simply admire horses. We love them.

Maybe you're lucky enough to ride regularly at a stable. Or maybe you've realized your dream and own your own horse. Or maybe you don't ride horses at all, but you think about them constantly.

That makes you part of a select group of people: horse lovers. And if you're at all like me, which I'm guessing you are, more than anything, you'd like horses to love you back. You want the ability to be good with horses. *Great* with horses.

We hear a good deal about horse whisperers, like Monty Roberts, or horse gentlers and trainers, like John Lyons, Pat Parelli, Cherry Hill, John Lyons, Mark Rashid, Linda Tellington-Jones, and others. They have different techniques, but the good ones have one thing in common. They pay close attention to the horses they train, taking into account the horse's nature, motives, needs, and desires.

Horse and human form a friendship based on mutual respect.

People who form solid relationships with horses end up with horses who want to please them.

I suppose I was a kind of horse whisperer before the term became so popular. But so were most of my friends, growing up in my small town, Hamilton, Missouri. Nobody wrote books about us or took our pictures. We had "backyard horses," kept in pastures behind our houses, or in barns and pens next to our homes. Our horses were rarely horse show material, but they proved to be great friends. If we couldn't ride every morning before school, we at least went out and greeted our friends in the barn before the bus came. And we rode a lot. But even more than that, we simply hung out with our horses.

I can't remember a time when my sister and I didn't have at least one or two horses. We learned from all of them. They became our teachers. My first "teacher," a pinto mare named Sugar, gave me the gift of my first solo ride when I was three years old. About a year later, she also presented me with my first fall.

Angel, our buckskin mare's first colt, taught me how to start a foal and train him to lead and ride. Angel also gave me my first serious bite, and biting became a habit Angel and I had to unlearn.

Misty, a black mixed Morgan, taught me the art of friendship. The gentle gelding listened to my problems every day after elementary school. Misty and I ventured into 4-H Horsemanship, where we both learned a lot about proper Western and English riding (since I'd mostly ridden bareback before).

When I was in high school, I got an amazing Appaloosa, Towaco, who won all kinds of regional competitions. Lancer, Butch, Rocket, Cindy, Seabreeze, Ash Bill, Moby, Cheyenne—they've all given me countless insights into horses, and into friendship.

You and Your Horse contains observations and facts horses probably wish humans understood. That's what this book is all about, building the right kind of relationship with horses, becoming friends.

Most good friendships take time. At school you might connect with someone because you share interests or hate the same classes. Your relationship grows as you begin to understand and trust each other. You develop inside jokes, laughing at things no one else gets. Pretty soon you know what the other person is thinking. Mutual respect, caring, and love have to follow if you're to be best friends.

I'm still learning from our horses. I spend most of my time writing, often writing about horses, horse lovers, and teen horse whisperers. In writing *You and Your Horse,* I've relied on experience and research. The secrets I'm sharing aren't magic. They're not even secret . . . if you have the kind of time it takes to study horses.

Unfortunately, not everyone is able to spend that kind

of time observing the world of horses. If you could—if you could spend days and hours, months and years, watching the way horses interact—you'd probably come up with these secrets on your own.

I'm just giving you a leg up.

There's a wonderful world of horses waiting for you. My hope is that you'll find, with a few changes in the way you interact with horses, that you can make friends with most of the horses out there.

Note to Readers: *You and Your Horse* is not intended to serve as a training manual, or to take the place of a good riding instructor. In all matters dealing with horses, the reader should keep in mind that safety comes first. Listen to the people in charge of the horses you visit and ride.

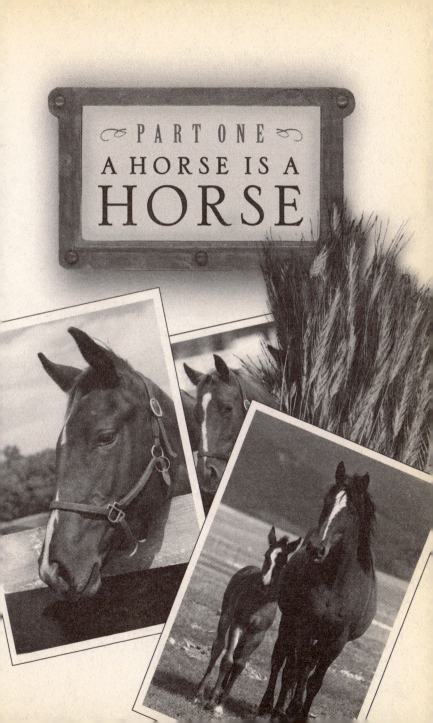

PART ONE
A HORSE IS A
HORSE

1

The Nature of Horses

To become a horse's friend and ally, we need to understand where horses are coming from. Even if your horse was born and raised in a stable, he'll still come equipped with instincts that would have helped him survive in the wild.

If you can understand what makes a horse a horse, you won't get so frustrated when he doesn't act like your neighbor or your best buddy. If you want a horse to fit into your world, you have to figure out how to fit into his.

Hunter or Hunted

Animals in the wild fall into two categories: hunters and hunted, or predators and prey. It's not exactly like bad guys and good guys, although it may feel like that to the hunted. The system works, with some animals on the prowl and others always on the lookout. But if you're in the "hunted" category, you know that at any moment, you could become somebody's dinner.

Horses are prey. They are the hunted. Once you get hold of that mind-set, what it's like to be a horse, you can begin to empathize and understand the nature of the horse. No wonder they can be jumpy. No wonder they get startled by loud noises and unexpected sights, even miles away. When you're the hunted, you can't be too careful.

You: The Hunter

Nobody really knows what horses are thinking. But on some level, they must consider us hunters, or predators. After all, we walk, talk, move, and smell like predators.

What can you do to change a horse's mind about the threat you pose to him?

- Relax. The calmer you are, the calmer your horse will be.
- Don't make any sudden movements. If you run at a horse, or jerk your arms, you make yourself into someone who needs to be watched.
- Talk in a smooth tone. Loud voices, like loud noises, make a horse want to keep her distance from you.
- Be dependable and consistent. Just because you're in a hurry or you've had a bad day, don't take it out on your horse. Be predictable.
- Be as horselike as you can. Watch how horses greet each other. Scratch your horse instead of patting him.
- Enjoy the companionship of your horse. Play, laugh. Horses love laughter!

• • • •

Your Horse: The Hunted

Think about it. Have you ever seen a horse do something that seemed crazy? A mare peacefully grazing in the pasture takes off running when you walk up. You're on a leisurely trail ride, and suddenly your horse bolts at nothing. You're riding in the same arena you always ride in, but someone's left a saddle pad over the rail, and your horse refuses to go past it. You're on a ride, and for no good reason, your mount takes off with you.

Crazy? Or horse nature?

Most horses aren't crazy. In fact, they like peace and quiet and goodwill. They're not fighters by nature. So when they're frightened, when they sense potential danger or run into something they can't understand, their best defense is to run like crazy.

Think like your horse. Talk to her from the second you enter the barn. As you move around your horse, keep one hand on her, gently, so she knows where you are. Don't sneak up on a horse. Horses don't like surprises.

If someone, or something, threatens you in a dark alley, what are you going to do? Run! If you were in the jungles of Africa, where you know lions abound, and you heard a noise in a bush, wouldn't you get out of there as fast as you could?

That's what it feels like to be prey instead of predator, hunted instead of hunter.

Dogs and cats don't have the same fear response that horses do. If your dog hears a loud noise or sees a rustling in the bush, he'll probably stop and crouch, ready to pounce and attack. He might bark at it. Or he may simply be curious and go investigate. Cats react the same way, most of the time. They might take off, but they may crouch in attack mode too.

Horses, on the other hand, run. Running away is a horse's natural response to fear. You can't determine what scares your horse when you're on a ride. The cause might be the flutter of a flag, or a squirrel leaping from tree to tree. Or it might be you, slipping off balance when you're on his back.

Horses rarely run for fun, and seldom or never out of malice. Their natural gait is a walk. If a horse takes off with you, assume she's afraid. Your job is to slow her down and bring her to a stop, then help her through her fear. Don't force your horse through a fear. Let her investigate and become convinced that she'll be okay.

Horses always have good reasons for doing what they do. It's up to us to figure out those reasons and offer help. Stay calm when your horse shows signs of fright, and he'll come to rely on you for safety. Understanding that your horse is afraid, and not ornery or scheming to make your life miserable, can open the possibility of a solid relationship between the two of you.

NATIVE AMERICANS AND THEIR HORSES

Native Americans valued their horses so much that war ponies were sometimes brought into a warrior's dwelling when the weather was bad. Wives and kids, of course, had to find somewhere else to sleep.

2

HERD MENTALITY

THE IN CROWD

If you could hang out in one of the few regions where mustangs still run wild, you'd see that horses weren't born to be loners. They eat, sleep, drink, and run in herds. Herds offer security and protection. For prey, there's safety in numbers.

Observe stable horses out in the pasture, and you can pick up some of the herd mentality that exists even in domesticated horses. Horses like to hang in small groups, pretty much like cliques at most schools.

Imagine the world through the eyes of a herd animal, a horse placed in a single stall, instead of in a field with other horses. Wouldn't it be natural to want out of that stall? To long for companionship? And if someone made

WHAT DO HERDS OF HORSES AND CLIQUES OF CLASSMATES HAVE IN COMMON?

- The group is controlled by a dominant female.
- The others in the group are basically followers.
- There's a definite pecking order, with some members considered more important than others.

• • CONTINUED ON P. 12 • • ☞

you leave all the other horses at the barn, wouldn't you hate to go, then wait for the opportunity to rush back?

Understanding that your horse would rather be in a herd might help you make his life a little better, and safer. Here are some tips:

• Whenever possible, let your horse hang out with other horses she's used to.
• If your horse is confined to a stall, turn her out as often as possible.
• Make sure that your horse can at least see other horses or animals or people, so she won't feel isolated.
• Understand that your horse will bond with other horses in your barn. That's why she may dog it on the ride out, away from the barn, and try to run all the way home. Stay in control, but recognize where she's coming from.
• If your horse can't seek the solace of a herd, she might replace the sense of home and security

with her stall. It's good to be aware of the draw of "home" on a horse. Some horses run to their stalls for safety, even when the barn is on fire and they're running back into the flames.

Horses are social creatures. Herds give them a sense of belonging. And like most of us, they want to know where they stand in relation to their peers.

Pecking Order

Horses find security and comfort in knowing their roles in the herd. It's not hard to identify the herd's dominant mare, the leader of the pack. Even when a stallion reigns as king, protecting and defending the herd, the dominant mare is usually the real leader. She's the one the others choose to follow. They keep an eye on her and try to please her and not get her riled. Another name for the dominant horse is the *alpha*.

The alpha horse calls the shots. She determines where the herd will go, where they can and can't eat. She gets first dibs on food and water, too. If you watch a group of horses that are fed at the same time, you can pick out the dominant mare. She'll be the one with her ears back, warning the others to stay away until she gets hers.

Pecking order has consequences. If a pesky mare decides she wants to go her own way and not follow the herd, the dominant mare will shut her out. For a social, prey animal, being excommunicated is a stiff price to pay.

If she's driven from the herd, she'll feel vulnerable and alone.

The whole system may sound callous, but having a pecking order gives all the horses in the herd a lifestyle they can count on. And that means security and contentment.

The longer you watch horses interact, the easier it is to pick out the pecking order. Who gets to eat and drink first? Which horse seems to be watched by the others? Keep an eye on personal space. Do some horses let any horse walk up and graze beside them? How close do they stand?

The pecking order in a herd continues to the bottom horse. If you feed five horses at once, you'll see the pecking order in action. The dominant horse, the alpha, gets first dibs. And when she's finished her own feed, she goes to another horse's bucket and finishes that, with no fight from the second horse. Unless that second horse is at the bottom of the pecking order, he'll move to a third horse's food bucket. And so on down the line . . . which is a good reason to develop a better feeding system than the free-for-all.

When you turn out a new horse into a pasture with a horse who's been around for a while, chances are sparks will fly. There could be biting, kicking, rearing, and worse. It's a good idea to set out bales of hay at opposite ends of the pasture, so horses can keep their distance and size up the newcomer while working out the pecking order. Above all, make sure the pasture is big enough to let the new horse do what he does best—run away.

3

A Herd of Two

Where do you fit in with the day-to-day life of your horse?

No matter how your horse relates to her horse buddies, she still needs to know where she stands when she's with you. You and your horse, or the horse you hang out with or ride, form your own herd of two, whether or not you realize it.

If you understand that you're part of a herd with your horse, then you can see yourself and your relationship in much the same way your horse perceives things. Wherever you have two horses, one needs to be the leader. If you don't take leadership, your horse will.

YOUR ALPHA ROLE

Your goal in your herd of two is to be seen as the alpha horse. Some horse people prefer to be considered a middle leader, rather than an alpha. But the important point is that you need to be higher than your horse in the pecking order.

You want your horse to look to you for leadership, to trust you to guide him.

Before you get too bossy, make sure you understand the pecking order from the horse's point of view. Dominant mares don't lead by force. Clearly, you don't want to lead by force, even if you could succeed in pushing around a thousand-pound horse. Being dominant never means abusing or mistreating your horse. The best alphas are gentle. Other horses submit to them because they trust their leadership.

Alphas lead with wisdom and dependability. They earn the role through making wise, consistent choices for

the good of the herd. Horses seek leadership. You need to earn your horse's respect so she'll accept you as her leader. That's where a healthy relationship with a horse begins.

Where do you stand now? Chances are, if your horse pushes you around, greets you with ears flat back and tail down tight, he thinks of you as lower in the pecking order than he is.

Signs of a horse submitting to your leadership include dropping his head, turning toward you, chewing—in a sense, asking permission. Later in this book we'll look at exercises that use horse language and signals to establish a healthy pecking order for you and your horse. Using nonthreatening but assertive postures with your horse in a round pen, for example, may help get you a higher ranking and more respect as a leader.

But here are a few tips for now:

- Show that you're the leader—not with force, but with confidence. Know where you want to go and what you want from your horse.
- Use a calm, firm tone of voice. Talk to your horse enough so that she'll recognize your voice and change of tone.
- Be calm. Don't freak out if your horse shies at a barking dog. Show your horse that you're not afraid. Talk and walk him through it.
- Be consistent. Don't let your horse get away

with something on Monday and then get mad at her for doing the same thing on Wednesday.

- Be alert. If you slack off, your horse might try to improve his position in the herd of two.
- Be patient. Earn and keep your horse's trust. Show her you're not afraid to do the spooky activity she's afraid to do—go into a trailer, cross a ditch or stream. Instead of forcing or punishing your horse, demonstrate bravery. Walk into the trailer first. Dismount and walk across the ditch before your horse, then with her. Patience earns trust.

GOOD AND BAD ALPHA TEACHERS

For insight into what will make you a good alpha leader, think about what makes teachers good . . . or bad.

GOOD TEACHERS	POOR TEACHERS
Give clear assignments	Give unclear assignments
Are fair and consistent	Are unfair and unpredictable
Are respected and respectful	Are intolerant and rude
Are patient	Are impatient
Make learning fun	Make you dread school
Build confidence	Make you nervous
Are easy to talk to	Never understand

- Be someone your horse looks forward to hanging with. Scratch him where he itches. Sing, play, have fun. Be fun!

Your alpha role needs to emerge from mutual respect. And when the roles are clear, life within your herd of two will be calmer and more fun for both of you.

SHARING WORLDS

Understanding the nature of horses you meet, horses you ride, horses you love, can make every horse experience better. If the horse runs away from you, it doesn't mean she hates you. She's following her nature to fear new things. (Later on, though, we'll look at some horse-friendly ways to catch that horse and to get her to want to come to you.)

If you keep in mind that a horse is a horse, and not a bigger version of you, your relationship should go more smoothly. The stable horse who decides he only wants to walk in slow motion this afternoon honestly doesn't realize that you're in a super hurry because you're getting picked up in thirty minutes.

The horse who balks at being loaded into a trailer, or puts up a fuss when you try to put him in a new stall, probably isn't launching an elaborate and well-thought-out plan or protest. He's scared. Going into an enclosed space takes away his single best weapon against fear—he can't run away.

If horses controlled their own world, they would never have anything on their backs or heads. They'd walk about freely, seldom trotting, and running only when afraid. They'd spend most of the day eating and grazing, then sleep out under the stars with their herd.

Horses have given up a lot to join our world. Try to see the world from a horse's point of view, and you and your horse will both be happier.

PART TWO
HORSE
SENSE

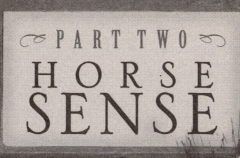

Horses have five senses, just like we do. But if we believe that they see, hear, feel, taste, and smell the way we do, we'll never understand the world of the horse.

As we come to appreciate the differences in how horses see objects, how they process sounds, smells, tastes, and touches, we can forge solid relationships, built on understanding and trust.

Makes sense, don't you think?

4

THE EYES HAVE IT

"MY, WHAT BIG EYES YOU HAVE!"

Horses have the biggest eyes of any land mammal. I love their large, soulful, expressive eyes. Sight is a vital sense to a horse. The hunted has to keep an eye out for the hunter.

Because those great big beautiful eyes sit on the sides of a horse's head, he's able to see in a circle, almost 360 degrees.

"THE BETTER TO SEE YOU WITH . . . SOMETIMES."

True, horses have two eyes just like us. But there the similarity ends. Like most hunters, or predators, humans have eyes in the front of the head. We have strong depth perception because our two eyes work together.

Horses, on the other hand, have eyes set on the sides of the head. In certain circumstances, they can see the same object with both eyes, the way we do. But more often, they see separate objects with each eye.

Because horses' eyes are farther apart than our eyes, they can't always focus as we do. A horse may need to raise or lower his head to study an object in his field of vision.

Another difference in the way horses see their world has to do with depth perception. Horses see in more places than we do. But since their eyes aren't positioned to work together, their depth perception may be different from ours. We might clearly see that there are two men in front of us while a horse might perceive the men as one big, scary object.

Horses are attuned to catch the slightest movement, but they may not see enough detail to know if what they're viewing is friend or foe. So the flutter of a flag in the distance startles your horse, and you're left wondering why she shied "at nothing."

Blind Spots

Remember how I said horses can see almost a full circle around them, almost 360 degrees? A horse can see possibly 340 degrees around her, which is a lot more than you can see around you. She sees you with her left eye when you're cleaning her left hind hoof. She keeps the right eye on you when you're brushing her right flank.

When horses graze, they can see most of what's going on around them. But—and this is a big "but"—they can't see *all* the way around them.

Horses have two troubling blind spots. One narrow blind spot is directly behind the horse. The other is directly in front. Both are important to understand if you want to maintain a good relationship with horses.

Looking Back

Why is it important to remember what horses can, and can't, see behind them?

- What a horse can't see, he fears. If you're riding, and your horse hears or senses something behind him but can't see it, he may not be comfortable until he can get to where he can see this threatening object.

- You want to go forward, but your horse starts dancing sideways. Consider the possibility that she is worried about something she can't see behind her. You might want to let her turn and see for herself that all is well.

- When you're on a trail ride and the horse behind you crowds, that horse will move out of your horse's field of vision. Anticipate trouble. Ask the other guy to please stay back, if you can't move forward.

- Your horse is grazing in the pasture. You're so happy to see her that you run up to her. But you're behind her, out of her field of vision. Bad scenario. Remember, no matter how much your horse loves you, anything out of sight is threatening.

- Think like your horse, and you'll be safer. If you're riding and you hear a loud noise behind you, know that your horse might react in fear.

He might kick at the unseen terror, or run from it, or try to wheel around and see for himself.

- When you're on your horse's back, she can see part of you, but not all of you. Her vision may allow her to see whatever you're carrying, a crop, the reins. So be careful how you move those objects.

- When you groom your horse and move around him, don't forget that he has a blind spot directly behind his hindquarters. Talk to him as you move around behind him, and don't hang out there!

EYES FRONT

As important as it is to keep in mind that horses can't see directly in back of them, it may be even more important to understand the blind spot directly in front of them.

- Horses can't see what's right under their noses. And yet that's where most people try to form a friendship with a horse, standing directly in front and under the nose—not a good idea. Stand to the side of your horse, where she can see you.

- Horses tend to lower their heads to see objects that are far away. And they tend to raise their heads to see close-up objects. If you approach your horse from the front, anticipate a head raise.

isn't able to track the source of the sound, the noise will be even more unnerving.

- Take into account the wind factor. Horses feel high-spirited in a strong wind. Part of the reason is that the sound of the wind rushing in their ears makes it harder for them to hear. They may see leaves and limbs blowing, but not be able to fix sound with sight.

On the other hand, take advantage of your horse's good hearing.

- Talk to your horse. Horses can pick out our voices, tones, and words.
- Use soothing tones. If you shout, that shout will sound louder to your horse.
- Develop a consistent horse vocabulary. Don't say "tee-rott" one day, then "Trot, trot, trot" the next. Use word cues for the other gaits: "Walk on," "Canter." Decide if you're going to say "Whoa" or "Stop." If you do say "Whoa," you might want to rid your horse vocabulary of "No." Sounds too similar, even to a horse.
- Talk to your horse as you groom her. Then she'll always know where you are.
- When I call my horse, Cheyenne, I say her name in the same way. She stops grazing, and her head snaps up long before she sees me coming.

6

HORSES HAVE GOOD TASTE

Taste, smell, and touch are connected for the horse. All three senses center around the muzzle.

TASTE GOOD?

Horses taste in much the same way we do, through taste buds on the tongue, although they also have taste buds around the palate and throat.

These taste buds help them separate flavors—salty, bitter, sour, and sweet. Taste and texture of food are important to a horse.

Horses like salt, and that innate fondness helps them get the nutrients they need. Stick a salt block where a horse can lick it freely, and she'll get her daily requirement of salt.

Horses tend to dislike anything bitter, which is a good thing. Most poisonous grasses and weeds are bitter, and horses tend to leave them alone. Unfortunately, horses can also choose to leave good-for-them medicines alone too, even when a pill is ground finely and mixed with feed. Most horses are skillful in using their lips to weed out the unwanted medicine and eat only the yummy grain.

But horses do have a sweet tooth. I've never met a horse

that didn't love molasses. Mix the ground-up medicine with molasses before stirring in the grain, and chances are that your horse will bite.

TASTING DANGER

Discriminating taste, plus a refined sense of smell, might keep your horse from eating sour feed or drinking bad water.

But maybe not. Misty, my best friend, the horse I owned during my elementary school years, died from eating insulation materials left in his pen by a careless plumber.

Horses can't vomit. This fact accounts for many deaths in horses. People, dogs, cats, and many other creatures can eat something bad and have a chance of hurling the poison out of the system and being okay again. Horses don't get that chance.

We need to look out for our horses and check everything they might put into their mouths.

Horses look strong and tough, but their stomachs make them vulnerable to colic. Colic means abdominal pain, a stomachache. Horses can get stomachaches for a variety of reasons. Remember, what goes in can't be thrown up. If your horse shows signs of a stomachache, call your vet immediately.

Some signs that your horse might have a stomachache are:

- She refuses to eat. (Most horses are good eaters unless something is wrong.)

- She keeps staring back at her side, as if a horse-fly were biting there.
- She's sweaty for no good reason.
- Her lips feel cool to the touch, especially on the inside of her mouth.
- Her pulse rate speeds up.
- Her breathing is irregular.
- She sways or tries to stretch out.
- She nips her side and shows signs of anxiety.
- Not understanding what's going on inside her, or what's causing the pain, the horse could paw with her forelegs or stomp her feet.
- Horses with severe stomach pain sometimes try to kick their bellies with their back legs.
- Horses with colic may try to lie down and roll over. Do your best to prevent that. A horse can tangle her intestines, making things much worse.

As your horse's leader, you're responsible for keeping her safe. Check her environment for anything that might cause trouble. Make sure she never has unlimited access to grain. If horses like the taste of a food, they will generally keep eating until they get sick. Horses that break loose and find their way to the feed bins or silos are almost sure to founder. Some horses may even eat themselves to death. They don't have shutoff valves in their stomachs.

You are your horse's shutoff valve.

Likes and Dislikes

So what do horses like? Grass, obviously. Hay, which can be grass hay or the higher-calorie kinds of hay, like alfalfa or clover. Grains, like oats, barley, or corn. And treats.

Horse owners report a variety of favorite horse treats. Apple slices were our first American Saddlebred's favorite. But our next American Saddlebred stuck up her nose at apples.

Most, but not all, horses enjoy carrots. My Morgan, Misty, didn't like those good-for-you orange veggies. He loved sugar cubes, but they weren't a good choice—too fattening. (Yep, even geldings have to watch their weight.)

Cheyenne, our paint, will do almost anything for watermelon rinds, but Moby, our white quarter horse, hated rinds.

Part of the fun of developing a friendship with a horse is discovering likes and dislikes. Try fruits and veggies first, though, and save the sugar cubes for special occasions.

Eating Out of Your Hand—or Not

Horse lovers can argue for hours about the wisdom of feeding a horse from your hand. The smart move is probably not to do it. You risk setting up your horse's expectations, which means you're bound to disappoint sometimes.

Many horse handlers believe feeding a horse by hand is asking to get bitten. Remember that horses have a blind spot right under their noses. They may not be able to tell if you have anything in your hand.

On the other hand, I have to admit that I like holding out a carrot for a trustworthy horse, or surprising her with oats held in the flat palm of my hand. I guess I can't help myself. I've always fed my horses by hand. And I've only been bitten by one horse because of it. That was Angel, the colt. And I'm pretty sure he would have bitten me anyway. I loved that little colt, but he never quite lived up to his name.

In defense of my hand-feeding, I don't hand-feed every time I show up at the barn. This cuts down on the expectation. And sometimes I do drop the handful of oats into the feed trough instead. I'd also never hide food in my pocket or try to get my horse to pull a carrot out of my jeans pocket. That would be asking for trouble.

Talk with the people who help or work with your horse. You don't want to start hand-feeding a horse someone else is working hard not to feed by hand.

UNDERSTANDING TASTE

I think the horse sense that has the most in common with our sense is taste. A horse's sense of taste is well developed and used mainly for deciding what's good to eat. You and your horse can both tell if something is salty or bitter, sour or sweet. And, like most horses, you probably vote for salty or sweet most of the time. You may even like some of the same foods, even food that's not good for you.

Watch out for your horse's diet as you watch out for your own.

7

THE SMELL OF HORSE

I love the smell of horse. I remember coming home from junior high, weighed down by some injustice or frustration, and rushing straight for the barn or pasture. I'd put my arms around my Appy's neck, bury my face in his mane, and inhale. Life would almost instantly return to normal.

Even today, as I'm writing this book, I'm looking forward to my end-of-the-day reward. I'll walk out to the field, get close to Cheyenne, and breathe deeply. Is there a better smell in the whole world? (And yes, I even love the smell of horse manure—not cow or pig manure, of course. But there's something about that horse manure . . .)

THE SENSE OF SMELL

The sense of smell is vital to a horse. Horses can smell a hundred times better than we can. Compare your horse's nose to yours. Horses have long faces with large nostrils. Watch the way those nostrils go in and out to capture scent and analyze it. You might see a horse breathe in deeply to get a better whiff. This big breath, through the nose and not the mouth, brings in more air with more information about the world. Scent messages are everywhere for the horse. Smell is how horses identify other horses, predators, food, life, and you.

The Jacobson's Organ

Horses have a special hollowing of the nasal cavity, called the *Jacobson's organ*, that can alert them to strange, and sometimes sexual, scents. If you've ever seen a stallion who's hot to trot over a brood-mare, you may have seen a *flehmen* response. It looks like a horse laugh, with the upper lip rolled back. The horse inhales to get a better scent to the Jacobson's organ.

Cheyenne curls her top lip whenever she smells something she doesn't like, especially medicine.

Social Smelling

Horses use their sense of smell in relating to one another. Mares depend on smell to recognize their foals. Horses in the wild use scent to locate their home herd.

Horses are always sizing up the world around them, categorizing friend or foe through the process of smell.

Seabreeze was the most high-strung horse we ever owned. Any new object in her line of sight had to be thoroughly sniffed or she couldn't go on. Like most horses, she hated the smell of death, even the death of a sparrow. After a while I came to realize that the mare wasn't frightened of every bush in the pasture. She just knew that something, at some time, had died there.

Ash Bill, a lovely and loyal chestnut quarter horse, rode like a dream for anyone who loved to ride, even if they weren't super riders. But he grew nervous with nervous riders. Horses can smell fear.

Watch horses introduce themselves for the first time. A common greeting is an exchange of breath—I'll blow in your nostrils, and you blow in mine. The exchange of breath allows the smell to travel deeply into a horse's sensory system.

Horses identify one another through smell. That's how they recognize horses that have proven to be friends a long time in the past. They store the memory of smells.

One of the reasons a horse feels at home in her own stall, rather than in the stall next door, is because her stall smells like her. And of all the smells in the world, a horse loves her own smell best.

Taking Advantage of Smell

Our sense of smell is so underdeveloped that we forget how important it is for a horse to be able to smell the world. How many times have you seen a horse stretch out her neck and point toward a new object, or toward you? Learn to take advantage of your horse's need to smell.

One of my favorite horse secrets came from watching the way Cheyenne and Moby greeted each other when I'd had one of them out for a ride. They blew into each other's nostrils. I started greeting my horses the same way. Cheyenne immediately returned the gesture by blowing back at me. Now we exchange this greeting a couple of times a week. Makes me feel loved.

Moby never did return my affectionate nose blowing. But we worked out another greeting we both came to enjoy. I'd stick out my hand, palm down, and she'd sniff it. Some days Moby would take her time and sniff hand, wrist, and upper arm.

Here are some good smelling tips:

- Give your horse time to really pick up your scent—not just once, but every time you come to visit. Slow down. Let him get a real whiff. After Towaco sniffed the back of my hand, sometimes I'd circle my finger gently inside one of his nostrils, giving him a deep sense of my smell.

- If you're riding and your horse lifts his head and stretches his neck, then sniffs or inhales and snorts, be on guard. He may have smelled something he doesn't like.

- Pay attention to your horse if you sense she's

anxious in the barn. Is there a new smell around? Some horses hate the smell of pigs, for example. Others are put off when there's a change in the composition of their water or feed.

- Remember that your horse recognizes your smell. Don't confuse him by using a new perfume. Human predator/hunter that you are, you will never smell as good to your horse as another horse would. But do the best you can.

- Horses like the familiarity of their own smell. Let your horse smell her blanket or saddle pad before you put it on her back. She'll recognize her own scent and be less likely to mind.

- If you're moving your horse, or traveling, take along familiar objects that carry his scent and remind him of home.

8

GET IN TOUCH

Horses have a much sharper sense of touch than we do. They feel with their entire bodies. Mares communicate and bond with their foals through smell and touch. Horses seem to be happier when they can see and touch other horses.

THE FULL-BODY TOUCH

When I was a freshman in high school, I went through an English-riding phase. I read books on how to show three-gaited and five-gaited horses. I followed the rules, which included trimming the horse for the best "show appearance." I clipped Cindy's and Seabreeze's ears and shaved their whiskers, just like I was taught.

For two summers I showed in horse shows all over Missouri, including Kansas City's American Royal. I ended up with a dresser full of trophies and a wall of ribbons. I loved the experience and thought Cindy did too. But I never got as close to that horse as I did to others. I don't think she was as happy as our other horses, and I know Seabreeze wasn't.

There may have been many reasons Cindy never worked

out as a backyard horse. But one reason had to be a loss of sensitivity to touch. If I'd known then what I know now, I never would have shaved that horse.

Horses' whiskers are like antennae. They let the horse know what's going on right under his nose, since that's a big blind spot. With whiskers, a horse can better judge how far she is from another object or from the ground. She can figure out textures of grass and plants before taking a bite.

In addition to these chin whiskers, horses have sensitive hairs above their eyes, like long eyebrows. These eye hairs protect their eyes and keep out dust and foreign matter. The hairs also warn if something is too close to the eyes.

Horses are forgiving, and I'm pretty sure Cindy forgave me for shaving her whiskers. I'm not so sure I've forgiven myself, but I've never shaved another horse since.

Whiskers, or the lack of them, are not simply for show.

TOUCH IS SKIN DEEP

A horse's whole body can feel as sensitively as your fingertip can. Did you ever see a horse twitch a fly off his back? He uses the muscles under his skin to do that. A fifteen-hundred-pound horse can feel the tiny legs of a fly before the fly has time to bite.

Some of a horse's skin sensors are located inside the skin. They tip off the horse to inside discomfort and pain. Skin sensors send out warnings that it's getting too hot or too cold out there.

Thoroughbreds and Arabians have thinner skin than other breeds, making them extremely sensitive to touch. But all horses feel more acutely than we imagine. Ultrasensitive areas of the horse include the mouth and flank. People who yank on the reins or kick with sharp boots and spurs can inflict more pain than they realize.

A TOUCH OF MAGIC

A horse's sense of touch is what allows a good rider and a good companion horse to flow as one. A confident rider can come to feel a part of her horse. The rider's gentle touch, the slight pressure of hand, thigh, or knee, a minute shift in weight—all of these will be picked up by the horse, as if by magic.

When I was a kid and rode Misty all day, I was convinced that horse could read my mind. I'd decide to ride down to the pond, and he'd head there before I could lift a rein. I'd realize it was time to go back to the barn, and Misty would turn around. He read my cues before I felt them myself. But to me, it seemed like magic.

This kind of touch communication is what makes some people think horses have a sixth sense. I think it's really a keen fifth sense, the sense of touch.

TAKING ADVANTAGE OF TOUCH

Understanding how sensitive a horse is to touch can change the way you interact with your animal. Here are some tips.

• • • •

Don't

- Don't be rough! Pats feel like slaps to a sensitive horse. A kick hurts. Before you inflict pain on a horse for training or punishment, imagine that act multiplied by a hundred. That's how it will feel to your horse.

- Don't shave or cut the hairs at your horse's muzzle or around his eyes. Trust me. It's simply not worth it.

- Don't ride the bit. Remember how sensitive your horse's mouth is. There's a bit in there. Don't jerk or pull hard on the reins. Be sure to use the gentlest bit you can, such as a snaffle or broken bit, rather than a curb.

- Don't be in such a rush. Your horse needs to touch things to figure them out. Let him touch you. Let him nose around that other horse, the dog or cat that hangs out at the arena. Give him time to explore through his refined sense of touch.

- Don't be fussy. It's rained all night, and the pasture is yucky mud. It's the perfect time for your horse to roll. Let her roll. She needs to feel that mud squish all over her skin. You can learn a lot from watching a horse roll. Some horses have to roll over to the left and wiggle back and forth, then stand up and do the same thing on the other side. If your horse can roll all the way over, it shows that she's agile and flexible. Good for her!

Do

- Do take advantage of your horse's sensitivity to touch by touching her often and everywhere. Touch your horse all over, being extra gentle at the tender areas, such as the flanks and under-belly. You can get your horse used to so many objects, including saddle, bridle, blanket, and saddle pad, simply by touch.
- Do read up on horse training methods that encourage gentle pressure and release of pressure, as opposed to force.
- Do groom your horse as often as you can. What better way is there to touch and massage your horse?
- Do remember how sensitive a horse is to the slightest pressure and movement of the rider on her back. Ride with confidence and a light hand. Think where you want to go, and your horse will probably pick up on it.
- Do deepen your friendship with your horse by scratching him where it itches. Horses have "sweet spots," places like the top of the withers or the curve of the jaw, where they'll do just

about anything to get you to scratch. Even my colt, the ornery little Angel, would stand still all day as long as I kept scratching his rump. He'd sway with pleasure. Horses need to be scratched. If you're the one fulfilling that need, you'll be a good friend.

Maybe you've grown up in a family that's not very touchy-feely. You're uncomfortable when Aunt Elizabeth gives you a hug, or when Cousin Cody pats you on the back. Some people are shy or nervous when it comes to touching.

But if you want a deep friendship with a horse, you need to get over that human resistance to touch. Touch your horse whenever you can. Respect his sensitivity and fill his need to be loved and accepted through consistent and loving touch.

~ PART THREE ~
THE ART OF
COMMUNICATION

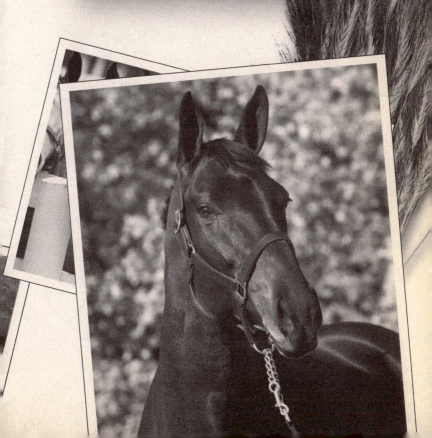

9

Horse Talk

Making Friends

Let's face it. It's not that easy to get to know a two-legged person your own age, same school, same town, who speaks the same language. You could spend every day of the school year with some kids and never know them well enough to communicate with them on a deep level—which explains the drama of throwing yourself on your bed and declaring, "Nobody understands me."

So how can you hope to communicate with a four-legged creature who weighs ten times as much as you do, lives in a barn, eats grass and hates pizza, and only speaks "horse"? We start by listening.

Straight from the Horse's Mouth

Horses do communicate verbally with one another. Listen to them. They may not use words, but their sounds can tell us a lot, if we're paying attention.

Horses make a wide range of sounds, but not every horse means the same thing by a neigh or a nicker. And even the same horse's nicker or neigh might have different meanings, depending on the circumstances. Your horse might nicker because she's glad to see you, or she may simply be telling you she's hungry.

In the next chapters, we'll bring into play a horse's expression and body language. But for now, here are some general interpretations of the vocalizations that horses make. Just remember that these are rough ideas, not language dictionaries. You'll have to pick up your horse's language by paying attention to him.

NEIGH: Your basic horse sound, a strong exhale, with voice to it. Horses neigh back and forth in horse dialogue. A neigh could be an announcement, a greeting, or a signal to the guys back at the barn: "Okay. I'm here."

WHINNY: A higher-pitched call than a neigh. The whinny is usually long and loud, with a question mark sound to it: "Hi! I'm over here. Is that you?"

NICKER: A low, rumbling sound a horse makes in his throat. It's my favorite sound in the world: "Great to see you, friend!" Or, "Got anything good to eat?"

When a mare nickers to her foal, it means, "Come here, sweetheart." Or, "Everything all right, love?"

SNORT: You snort, so you probably recognize this one, right? Horses make the sound by exhaling through the nostrils alone. The louder the snort, the more serious the cry. "Yikes! What's that?" Or a snort may warn another horse of danger. On the other hand, a snort could be saying, "Back off, man! My territory."

SQUEAL: A sharp exhale with a nasal quality. The squeal can be short or long. A stallion could be saying, "Don't take another step this way, or you'll be sorry!" Or, "That chick over there, I mean mare, is mine!"

A mare might let out a flirtatious squeal when a stallion advances on her.

SCREAM: I hope you never hear a horse make this high-pitched cry, a burst of terror from the lungs, usually caused by pain or anger. "Stop that! That hurts!" Or, "Now you've done it. Look out!"

Horse handlers identify other horse talk. Some refer to a "whicker," which seems to be a lot like a nicker. Others talk about the "whistle" a stallion uses to get a mare to come to him. There's a "squeak," which sounds like a cutoff squeal from an interested mare. And you'll hear "snuffles" and "sniffs" and different forms of "blowing," not to mention the grunts and groans you'll get when you're working your horse.

If you're listening, you'll learn your horse's own special verbal language. And you'll have taken another step toward becoming a good friend.

10

HORSE SIGNALS

Horses can use their voices in communicating with other horses and with us. But more often, they signal with their eyes and nostrils, their tails, their ears, and their entire bodies.

GESTURES

Nobody can tell you what your horse is saying. But if you spend time watching him, you'll start to understand. A neigh could have a dozen meanings, depending on inflection, tone, volume, and gestures.

But that's the way our language is too.

Think about how you use your own words. You could say, "Hey," in a short, friendly tone and mean, "Hi, buddy!" Or you might draw out the "Hey" in a low voice and mean, "You are so cute. Why don't you come over here and talk to me?" Or you could shout, "Hey!" when you're angry or surprised, or "Hey?" when you really mean, "What in the world do you think you're doing?" A good friend would pick up your meaning.

Be a good friend to your horse. Learn to understand his signals.

Body Language

Horses communicate with other horses through body movements. It pays to watch and learn horse body language.

- A dominant horse might resort to kicking a horse she thinks is encroaching on her space. It should be pretty obvious what's being said: "Take that!"
- Before one horse kicks another, the aggressive horse will probably swing his rump around as a warning. What better way is there to say, "Back off, man!"
- A swing of the horse's head may signal another horse to move away. Horses will bump one another for position too. They might try to bump you if they feel they're being crowded.
- An arched neck might just say, "Look how beautiful I am," or "I'm feeling fine!"
- Add tossing the head to that arched neck, and maybe throw in a tiny squeal of pleasure, and your horse is probably showing off and may be about to kick up her heels, shouting, "I'm feeling my oats and just may buck to prove it." It's a sight that's a joy to watch when the horse is in a pasture. But if you're on her back, you need to read the signs and head off disaster by changing directions, reining the arch out of her neck, or slowing down.

- If you're riding and your horse stretches his neck forward and ducks his head, he may want to go faster. But if he stretches his neck, ducks his head, then slows down, the bit might be too tight.
- A horse that's about to bolt, probably from fright, usually sends off signals first. She throws up her head, points her nose to the sky, and may give a tiny squeal. What do you do? Breathe, turn your horse, take control, talk calmly to her.
- Horses nip each other, and those nips might be affectionate, even flirtatious. You'll have to watch horses interact to figure out when horse biting is friendly, and when it's not.
- Horses stamp their feet for different reasons. They might be saying, "I don't like it here!" Or, "I've just about had all I can take of this." Or, "Can't we play or something? This is so bor-r-ring." On the other hand, it may be fly season.
- A raised back hoof might say, "I'm tired and relaxing." Or it might say, "Get ready! I'm about to kick."
- When you're on your horse's back, you can't see all the signals of communication, but you can feel them. If your horse tenses up, you should be able to sense it and help him through whatever's troubling him.

Tail Talk

Horses communicate volumes with their tails.
Here are some tips to get you started on observing and interpreting your horse's tail signals.

- *Tail held high:* "I'm proud to be a horse!
  I'm gorgeous! In fact, I'm so amazing
  that I might 'high-tail' it out of here!"
  This could be something you can sit back
  and enjoy from a distance as your horse
  runs in the pasture. But if you're riding,

you might want to be on the alert for bucks or a speedup.

- *Clamped-down tail:* "This is scary. Whatever's going on, I don't like it." When I'm riding Cheyenne, even with a Western saddle, I can feel her tail tighten, tuck, and clamp down. It's a cue for me to pay extra-close attention and try to figure out what she's afraid of.

- *One sharp, well-aimed tail swat:* "I hurt right there." Your horse's tail could be an early plea for help, if you're listening. On the other hand, she may be saying, "Got ya, fly!"

- *Tail switching hard and fast:* "I'm really angry, and you better stay out of my way." If you sense that tail swishing steadily back and forth when you're riding, make sure you're not doing anything to make your horse mad, like confusing him by being off balance.

• • • •

Be on the lookout for subtle body language. Some people only see the horse kick. Others, before they see the kick, notice the rump spin around, the weight shift off the kicking leg, and the ears flatten back. They'll see trouble coming and have a shot at heading it off.

Face It

Your horse's face will become more and more expressive the more time you spend with him. Pay attention to all the clues and cues given off at the front end of your horse.

Mouth

- A tight mouth (especially combined with narrow eyes) could be telling you that your horse is in a bad mood or in pain.
- A tight mouth, clamped shut while your horse is being saddled, may be telling you that you've been cinching that saddle too tight. Either that or your horse is simply outsmarting you, as nearly all of mine have outsmarted me. He's holding his breath so you can't cinch the saddle too tight.
- The mouth and lips give cues of submission. Licking the lips is a sign that your horse is letting you be the alpha. Many horse trainers pay great attention to the licking and chewing of a horse.
- If the lower lip is hanging, and it doesn't

When you saddle your horse, check and see if his lips are pressed together. If they are, lift the upper lip and see if the tongue is pressed against the teeth. If it is, your horse is holding his breath. You may think you're getting that saddle girth nice and tight . . . until you mount. Then the whole saddle could swing down.

normally hang, your horse is probably very relaxed.

- Some horses pout, or at least they look like they're pouting. Butch the Backing Wonder liked to stick his upper lip down whenever we tried to make him go forward.

- Tight lips with wrinkles around them tell you your horse is tense.

- Showing teeth and rolling back the upper lip shows sexual interest, or it might just mean your horse tasted something yucky.

- Showing teeth with ears back is your cue to get out of there. You're about to get bitten, or worse.

Look into Their Eyes

- Eyes wide open, with the white membrane showing, is a cue to you that your horse is nervous about something. If you see the whites of the eyes, be on guard.

- Horses get "worried wrinkles" around the

eyes when they're not comfortable.

- If your horse blinks more than usual, she's probably thinking harder than usual. She might be trying to make sense of something you just tried to show her.
- Narrow eyes may indicate pain or a bad mood.
- Observe those eyes, but don't stare directly into them. Staring is threatening to a horse.

Ear Talk

I've saved the most helpful horse language for last. Horses "talk" with their ears. The truth is, horses can say more with their ears than most people say with words.

Because horses' ears are flexible and rotate, the ears can send a variety of specific signals. Listen to your horse's ears.

- *Relaxed ears, aimed forward:*
  "Nice day, don't you think?"
  Generally, ears aimed forward, but loose and relaxed, mean your horse is in a good mood.
- *Ears flicking back and forth:*
  "I'm listening. I'm ready."
  If the ears are twitching and stiff, he might be saying, "I am so out of here!"

- *Pricked forward, stiff ears*:
  "What was that?"
  It could be that something has captured your horse's interest, and she's simply curious and on the alert. But ears pricked forward could also mean your horse is worried or fearful about something ahead. If her body stiffens, then you might want to turn your horse in another direction or be prepared to help her through whatever lies ahead.
- *Uneven ears, one up, one back:*
  "Anything interesting going on around here?"
  Or, if they move back and forth while you're riding: "I'm trying to listen to you, but I have to listen to what's out there, too, you know?"
- *Airplane ears, lopped to the sides:*
  "Yawn. Bor-ing."
- *Droopy ears:*
  "I'm sleepy." Or, "I don't feel so good."
- *Flat-back ears:*
  "You're making me angry!"

If your horse lays back ears flat against his head, that means trouble. Stay away if you're in biting or kicking range. This is one of the best signals you can learn to stay safe around horses. If you're riding, heads up. Your horse may be about to shy, balk, take off, or leap to the side.

- *Ears back, but not flat:* "What's going on back there?" It's good to know that when you're riding and your horse's ears turn back at you, you don't automatically have to assume that she is mad at you. She might simply be listening to you or to something else going on behind her.

Horses talk to us in many ways. You'll understand the language better if you consider the combination of signals your horse is giving off. Put it all together—body, ears, voice—the same way you do when you listen to humans, taking into account a person's tone, inflection, expression, and gestures.

11

COMMUNICATE YOURSELF

Communicating with horses is a two-way commitment. You need to listen and learn to read the signals your horse is giving you. But you always need to find ways to let him hear and understand what you're saying.

Horses are reading you all the time. Everything you do and say, don't do and don't say, will amount to communication with your horse. They hear what you say, even when you don't say it. They sense how you feel before *you* do.

Pay attention to yourself and the message you're sending. Communicate your best self to your horse. Whatever mood and character qualities you show to your horse will come right back at you.

A QUIET CONFIDENCE

Your horse needs you to feel confident when you're around her. Having confidence doesn't mean you're convinced you're the best cowgirl since Annie Oakley. It can be as simple as expecting things to turn out all right.

I've known several inexperienced, unlikely horse people who were still great with horses because they expected horses to like them. One six-year-old girl, who had never been around horses, walked right up to a hard-to-catch horse and got the old mare to follow her to the barn. When I asked her how she'd managed to get the mare to come in with her, the girl frowned and said, "Why wouldn't the horse want to come with me?" That innate, or maybe naive, confidence had been communicated to the mare.

Most of us need to work on our confidence, though. The more you watch horses and get to know your own horse, the more confident you'll feel around him. It's like taking a class. If you do the homework and listen to discussions, you have more confidence than if you just pay attention before the tests.

Have confidence in yourself and your horse—not that you're a great rider and have all the answers, but that you and your horse together will figure things out.

A KIND AND GENTLE SPIRIT

Half your battle in forming a relationship with your horse on any given day takes place before you get to the barn. If you're upset about other things, don't take it out on your horse.

In fact, if you let him, your horse will help you be a gentler person. Sometimes when I'm wound up from the frustrations of life, I leave my computer and walk to the barn or pasture. I know that thirty minutes of soaking up Cheyenne's gentle spirit will help me calm down.

A good ride does the same thing. When I focus on

Cheyenne and the beat of her hooves, the sway of her gait, all other thoughts take a backseat. I can sweep my mind of craziness, at least for as long as I'm riding.

Kindness goes a long way. If you don't know a thing about horses, but you're a kind and gentle person, you're well on your way to becoming a friend to horses. By nature, horses are kind. It's only when they're treated unkindly and harshly that they return the favor.

PATIENCE

Horses aren't in a hurry. Their natural gait is a walk. You may show up at the stable and want to squeeze in the most riding you can in that hour. But remember that your horse has all day. She won't understand why you're in such a rush. And she won't like it.

Take a deep breath. Take a lot of them. Relax and enjoy whatever time you have with that horse. Two minutes of companionship is better than two hours of conflict.

TRUSTWORTHINESS

Remember that your horse should look to you and know she can trust you. Can she count on you? When she sees something move up the road, can she tell you're okay with it, so she'll be okay too?

Horses grow to trust us the same way we come to trust our friends. I trust my best friend because she does what she says she'll do. If she tells me she'll feed the dogs and check on the horses for me when I'm out of town, I know

I won't have to worry about them when I'm gone. I've counted on her before, and she's come through for me. I also know that when I have a problem, I can come to my friend, and she'll be ready to help. We can talk about the problem together. And if she's convinced that the situation isn't as bad as I thought it was, I'll probably stop worrying so much.

Your horse would love to trust you. Prove you're trustworthy.

12

SPEAKING "HORSE"

We've already tried to analyze the way horses use their voices to talk to one another. They vocalize with nickers, neighs, whinnies, whickers, snorts, and quite a few other sounds.

I've never tried to imitate those sounds, but I do think horses learn to understand our sounds, and even our words.

CALM, LOW VOICE

A calm voice tells your horse that you're not afraid. You're someone he can depend on to guide him.

So what if you don't feel calm? What if that big dog ahead scares you as much as it scares your horse? Then breathe. Fake it. You can make your voice low and calm. It's not as good as being fearless, but it's better than fanning the flames of your horse's fear.

DON'T SHOUT

Shouting rarely helps your horse out of a jam. Instead, you'll only make things worse. And remember that his hearing is much better than yours. So a shout sounds like a SHOUT.

Talking on Your Feet vs. Talking in the Saddle

Grooming is a good opportunity for you to talk things over with your horse. Friendly chatting lets your horse keep track of you when you're on the ground. He can grow in understanding as he gets used to the sound of your voice.

But don't be too chatty in the saddle. It's hard for your horse to focus while in motion. If you're talking a blue streak, she'll have to listen to you and to everything else. Save your saddle talk for calming, rewarding, and giving cues.

Voice Cues

If you want your horse to learn a voice command or cue, expect to say that word hundreds of times. Say it in the same way, with the same inflection.

Maybe the most common horse-talk word you hear in a group of riders is "Whoa." If the word works for you and for your horse, that's great. That's all that matters, the communication between the two of you. But for me, "Whoa" sounds too much like "No" and "Go."

Word commands or voice cues that make sense to me are "Walk on!" "Tee-rot!" and "Canter." Each word can be said to sound like what you're asking your horse to do.

Laugh!

Use your voice to show your horse that you're a good time.

Laugh around your horse. Horses love laughter. Plus, it reminds you why you're bothering with horses in the first place. You love them, and they're fun.

13

Signaling "Horse"

We communicate with horses by communicating ourselves to them. And we'll communicate ourselves the most effectively when we talk like horses talk to one another—through voice, body language, and actions.

Actions Speak Louder Than Words

Don't forget that every action you take, or don't take, will communicate something to your horse.

Take good care of your horse. If you don't feed, water, groom, and attend to your horse, you're communicating that she's not that important to you.

Show up at the stable or barn or pasture when you don't want anything but companionship. You don't have to ride every time you see your horse. If all you do is work with your horse, you're clearly communicating that you only care about what the horse can do for you. You're not interested in friendship, and your horse won't be either.

The Things You Do

We'll look more closely at this one in a later chapter, but

what you do on the ground will communicate volumes to your horse. When you groom her, you'll be telling her whether you enjoy her company, or whether you're in a rush to move on to other things.

Sudden movements on the ground tell your horse that you're a predator and he'd better not trust you. Don't grab at your horse or stick your hand in his face. Don't run at him.

When you're in the saddle, you'll use words. But horses respond to the unspoken, too—a light increase or decrease in pressure, the lifting of a rein, the hint of a lean forward.

HANGING OUT IN THE HERD

Horses in a pasture or herd spend most of the day grazing together, with little direct interaction. I think they like the comfort of hanging out.

So hang out with your horse.

In sixth grade my teacher noticed that all my math papers smelled a little "funny." I disagreed. But the truth was that I did nearly every homework assignment sitting in the barn or out in the pasture with Misty.

I read my first Jane Austen novel in the middle of Towaco's pasture, while he grazed, ignoring me, but moving closer and closer.

On dozens of spring and fall mornings when I was in fourth grade, I'd pack up a quick breakfast and ride out on a country road. Then I'd slide off my horse, and we'd eat breakfast together—all before I had to go to school.

Be creative. Come up with new ways to spend time with the horse you love.

SHOWING LOVE

Communicate affection the way your horse likes it, not the way you do.

You may think you're saying, "I love you" when you rub your horse's muzzle or reach up to pat his head. But he's not hearing "I love you."

Instead, show affection the way horses show affection to one another. Rub and scratch. Be a good friend and try out different "sweet spots" until you find his favorites—under the mane, in front of the withers, under the chin, behind the jaw, on his cheek, on his chest or rump.

Scratch your horse where he itches, and he'll hear "I love you."

At least try exchanging breath the way horses greet horses. Blow gently into one nostril and see if you get a return greeting.

SHOWING RESPECT

Respect your horse the way horses respect one another.

Respect your horse's personal space. Remember her blind spots and stay out of them. Stand to the side of your horse, by the right or left shoulder. If a horse sneaks up on another horse from behind, he can expect to get kicked. So can you.

Announce yourself when you're intruding on your

horse's stall. Don't barge in. Talk to her and take your time. Be a good visitor and a great friend.

Horses need time to check you out, even when they already know you. Horses sniff horses all the time. They nuzzle one another. Give your horse that kind of time to get reacquainted.

If your horse brings his head around in your direction, it's a big compliment. Be grateful and respectful. Stand still, with your arms at your sides, and let your horse sniff you out. Be nuzzled. Don't interrupt the nuzzling because you're in a rush to give your horse a hug. You'll have time for that. Then, when your horse has satisfied his need to nuzzle, you can scratch, stroke, and hug, showing mutual respect.

PUTTING IT ALL TOGETHER

Horses use all parts of their bodies to communicate. So do you, whether you realize it or not. You're saying something all the time. And horses are skilled in listening to us.

If you don't say a word, but you're afraid of horses, they'll pick up on that. Then they might be scared of you, or try to boss you around. But if you're calm and confident, your horse will be calm and confident too. The communication you send will come back to you.

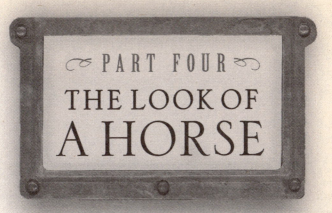

PART FOUR
THE LOOK OF A HORSE

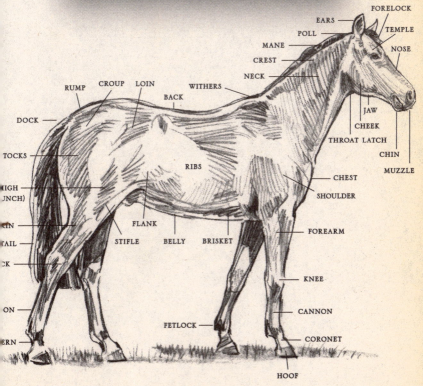

FORELOCK
EARS
POLL
TEMPLE
MANE
NOSE
CREST
NECK
WITHERS
BACK
JAW
LOIN
CHEEK
CROUP
RUMP
THROAT LATCH
CHIN
DOCK
MUZZLE
TOCKS
RIBS
CHEST
IGH
SHOULDER
UNCH)
IN
FLANK
FOREARM
AIL
STIFLE
BELLY
BRISKET
CK
KNEE
ON
CANNON
ERN
FETLOCK
CORONET
HOOF

14

Sizing Up Horses

Measuring Up

Horses are measured in *hands*. A hand is considered four inches (roughly the width of a cowpoke's hand). Height is measured from the highest point of the withers down. The withers form the high point of the back, at the base of the neck, located between the shoulder blades.

Height measurement for horses is written in hands and inches. So Towaco was 15.2, or 15 hands, two inches, or sixty-two inches from the withers. Cindy measured 17 hands, or sixty-eight inches.

Shetland ponies are around 10 hands high. The smallest horse breed is the Falabella from Argentina, averaging about thirty inches. Miniature horses can be dog-sized. The smallest living horse is Thumbelina, a miniature only seventeen inches high and weighing sixty pounds.

At the other end of the scale,

HORSE OR PONY?

The general rule is that 14.2 is the cutoff point in height, separating a horse from a pony. But breeds may vary on this and place more emphasis on looking like a pony or horse structurally.

shire draft horses can grow to 17 or 18 hands. Samson, a shire foaled in 1846, grew to 21.2 ½ hands, or more than seven feet high, and weighed in at more than 3,300 pounds.

HORSES' AGE AND GENDER

Horses are living longer and longer, thanks to good feed and great care. The average horse may live well into his twenties and even thirties. A few keep going into their forties. The oldest horse we know about was Old Billy, an English barge horse, who lived to age sixty-two.

Depending on the age and sex of the horse, horse people have developed a variety of ways to refer to their horses. Here are some of the terms you might hear tossed around at a stable or ranch.

FOAL: A foal is a baby horse, male or female. It takes about eleven months for a foal to be born. Officially, a horse is a foal if it's under one year old. If the foal is still nursing, it's sometimes called a *suckling*. If the foal no longer nurses but has been weaned away from its mother, it's called a *weanling*. Foals are usually weaned when they're around four to six months old.

YEARLING: A yearling is any horse, male or female, that's a year old—after his or her first birthday, but before the second birthday. Officially, all horses are considered to have been born on January 1 following their actual birth.

COLT: A colt is a male horse under four years old. Sometimes, since many people use the term *colt* for any young horse, a male horse of this age is referred to as a *horse colt*.

FILLY: A filly is a female horse under four years old. Fillies, like colts, grow fast. They reach their adult size in four or five years.

STALLION: Adult male horses are either stallions or geldings. A stallion is an adult male horse, age four years and older, who hasn't been *fixed* (also called *altered* or *castrated*). He is *ungelded,* unaltered so that he can still father foals. The father of a foal is called the *sire.* Stallions are usually kept by themselves because of their tendency to fight for dominance.

GELDING: A male horse that's been fixed is called a *gelding.* People may castrate a male horse because, generally, geldings are easier to take care of, better natured, and easier to ride and keep around other horses.

MARE: A mare is an adult female horse four years old or older. The mother of a foal is called the *dam.*

TELLING AGE BY A HORSE'S TEETH

It's true that you can estimate a horse's age by his teeth. But you need to understand the way a horse's teeth grow.

Milk Teeth

Some say a foal is born toothless and cuts milk teeth in about ten days. Others say the foal is born with two or three temporary molars in each side of the jaw. Milk teeth are small and pure white. The permanent teeth that replace milk teeth will be much darker. This color difference will be a big help in guessing a horse's age when the horse is still young.

Growing Up

- Six months to two years: At one year, the colt should have a complete set of twenty-four milk teeth, small, white, and smooth.

- Two to five years: If you think a horse is about two, check the front teeth (the incisors) to tell the age. Milk teeth are on their way out and will be gone by age five, and the horse should have a full set of permanent teeth—forty for males, thirty-six for females.

- Five to eight years: Starting at about age six, you can look at the lower incisors and see a cup, or pit, in the center of each incisor's flat surface. The incisors show changes with age. At six the cups have already started disappearing, and at nine, they're all gone. This is a hard age to sort out by teeth. But the teeth keep growing, so if they appear small, especially in the back, the horse is likely closer to five. If the teeth are large, he's probably closer to eight or nine.

- Nine to fifteen years: Teeth slant out toward the front. They begin to change shape. Ends of the teeth become rounder. After age eleven, teeth become more triangular, and stick out a bit toward the front of the mouth with each additional year.

THE GALVAYNE'S GROOVE

The Galvayne's groove is the easiest way to tell a horse's age after age ten. It's a dark, vertical line that will grow down the upper corner incisor, then recede back up.

- Age ten: The Galvayne's groove appears at the gum.
- Age fifteen: The Galvayne's groove is about halfway down the tooth.
- Age twenty: The groove reaches all the way down the tooth.
- Age twenty-five: The groove goes halfway up again.
- Age thirty: The groove has disappeared. So if you're looking at a tooth with no Galvayne's groove (and you're sure the horse isn't younger than ten), that horse is probably thirty years old or more.

• • • •

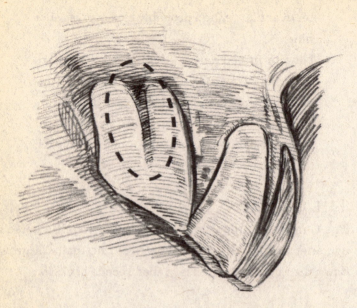

Unfortunately, even if you master the art of telling a horse's age by his teeth, there are horse traders out there who've mastered the art of filing a horse's teeth to make him appear younger.

15

CLASSIFYING HORSES

THE BIG PICTURE

A breed is a group of horses that share characteristics that can be inherited. If two Arabians get together, they'll have an Arabian that looks a lot like they do.

Depending on which book you trust, you can count more than three hundred breeds of horse.

HOT-, WARM-, AND COLD-BLOODED

I admit that I'm not a big fan of the terms horse people use when talking about breeds. They divide all horses into three categories: hot-bloods, cold-bloods, and warm-bloods. For me, it's a confusing way to group horses. Horses don't vary in body temperature according to breeds.

Some people use the terms to describe temperament. They'll call an Arabian or an American Saddlebred hot-blooded because they find those breeds more tightly wound than the laid-back workhorses they'll deem cold-blooded.

Here are some standard definitions for the terms:

- **Hot-blooded:** Arabians, barbs, and Thoroughbreds. Most of our breeds come from these older lines.
- **Cold-blooded:** Heavy European draft horses. Lighter horses were bred with these to develop more breeds.
- **Warm-blooded:** Everybody else. Combine hot and cold, and this is what you get. Many of these breeds were developed for specific purposes, like jumping, racing, pleasure riding, and eventing.

You can do your own study on the hundreds of horse breeds. Since this isn't a horse textbook, but a book about horse relationships, I'll just fill you in on some of the more common breeds, some of the breeds of horses I have known. And I'll extend my apologies if I've left out your favorite breed.

Horse Breeds I Have Known

Over the years I've met a lot of horses. I've never met a breed I didn't like, although I admit I do love some more than others.

American Quarter Horse

Considered the classic Western, or cowboy, horse, the quarter horse is easygoing and the fastest horse over a quarter mile. The chief characteristic of a quarter horse is a compact and well-muscled body. The result is a quick, sure-footed horse that's hardy but agile.

I love the nature of a good quarter horse. Ash Bill never got rattled at horse shows, on trail rides, or on back roads, no matter what happened. Moby, my second quarter horse, proved to be a great kid horse, while still giving grownups a fun ride. With roping, reining, ranch working, and simply being a family horse, this is the leading breed in the United States.

AMERICAN SADDLEBRED

American Saddlebreds range between 15 and 17 hands high. They are characteristically exquisite, alert and flashy, with big eyes and pointed ears set close together on a fine head. The neck is long and arched, and long legs strut and prance. Mainly show horses, refined and spirited, American Saddlebreds perform in three-gaited classes at a walk, trot, and canter, all arched and high stepping. And they may be shown as five-gaited horses, with an extra prancing "slow gait" and a full-speed "rack."

All three Saddlebreds I've

HOW FAST IS A HORSE?

• A good horse can gallop at twenty-five to thirty miles per hour (breaking city speed limits).
• A Thoroughbred might break forty miles per hour.
• A quarter horse, running a quarter mile, may hit fifty miles per hour (for short distances).

owned have been gorgeous to look at and fun to ride . . . most of the time. But they tended to shy at flags, barking dogs, and things I couldn't see.

ANDALUSIAN

This Spanish breed of horse averages 15 to 16 hands high, with a light build, low, rounded shoulders, and elegant lines. Andalusians are intelligent, lively, and showy. You might see an Andalusian in a parade, a horse show, a dressage performance, a circus, or even a bullfighting ring.

Every Andalusian I've glimpsed has stunned spectators with its noble presence, regal head, luxuriant and wavy mane and tail, and athletic grace.

APPALOOSA

Appaloosas were bred by the Nez Perce Native Americans for their spotted, dramatic coloring, their strong, muscular bodies, and their friendly disposition. A true Appaloosa will have a refined head and the characteristic coloring of the breed—spots, or mottled patterns. Other genetic markers include mottled skin, a mottling around the eye, with the white sclera visible, and striped hooves. They're known for good endurance and great temperaments.

Appaloosa coloring patterns include:

- *Blanket:* white over the hips, with or without dark spots.
- *Leopard:* white and dark spots (like a leopard).

- *Snowflake:* strong spotting over the hips.
- *Frost:* white speckling on a dark background.

My Towaco had a brown-and-white blanket pattern typical of the breed. His quarter horse temperament made him my best friend throughout high school.

ARABIAN

An Arabian is easy to recognize: chiseled head, dish jowls, giant eyes, arched neck, short back. Loaded with stamina and grace, the Arabian is beautiful. Although Arabians have a reputation for being high-spirited, they also have a reputation for making great friends with humans.

My best horse-loving friend in elementary school dreamed of owning an Arabian. Today she's living and riding that dream. And she swears that Arabians seek human friendship and make wonderful companions.

BELGIAN HORSE, OR BRABANT

Belgians are one of the strongest and heaviest breeds. They're workhorses, known for their patience, good nature, and hard work. They grow to an average of one ton—that's two thousand pounds—and stand over 17 hands tall. Belgians are generally a roan or light chestnut color, with a flaxen, wavy mane and tail.

Our Amish neighbors need big, reliable horses to plow their fields. I've never met a kinder horse than Bob, their gentle giant of a horse.

BUCKSKIN

The requirement for this breed is based on the cream-tan coloring, with black on the mane, tail, and lower legs. Some horses in the breed have a dorsal stripe down the spine. But breeders claim that in addition to the coloring, a buckskin's traits have been handed down through generations: strength, stamina, solid bone structure, hardiness. They say buckskins (and the breed includes duns, zebra duns, red duns, and grullos) are "tough as leather."

Rocket, the second horse we had growing up, was a good-natured horse who would gallop through the pasture all day—with my sister and me riding double. That mare was never injured or sick, and she delivered her foal without our help.

CLYDESDALE

The Clydesdale is a hardworking breed of draft horse characterized by its gigantic size. Clydesdales are usually 17 to 18 hands high, big boned, strong, and very heavy, often with white "boots" and long fetlocks. Yet they have a gentle look, with their big eyes and giant ears tuning in to everything around them. The breed originated from Clydesdale, Scotland, but gained notoriety as the giant horses pulling in TV ads for a beverage.

When I saw the famous Clydesdales in St. Louis, I couldn't believe how fast they moved or how big their hooves were.

CONNEMARA

Technically, the Connemara is a breed of riding pony, but Connemaras are about as tall as a "pony" gets, reaching a height of around 14.2 hands. With strong muscles and compact bodies, they make great jumpers. A native of Ireland, the Connemara is dependable and considered an all-purpose horse, as well as a child's pony.

I rode a Connemara when—on assignment to write an article for *Western Horseman*—I traveled to western Ireland, where the breed originated. My mount proved to be fast, agile, hardy, surefooted, and kind.

• • • •

Falabella

Falabella, a breed originating in Argentina and descended from the Andalusian, is the smallest horse breed in the world. It tops out at about 7 hands, too little to ride, but a great size for a pet. Unlike ponies, the Falabella is streamlined and can look like a Thoroughbred, an Arabian, a quarter horse, or any breed.

An animal-care training program near where I live keeps a cute Falabella as a pet, which is how the little horses were used for centuries. In addition, the animal-care students are able to learn proper grooming and handling with a horse that's only twenty-eight inches high, a horse they're not afraid to handle.

Hackney

The Hackney horse used to pull royal carriages in Great Britain. The breed's characteristics include stamina for traveling fast over great distances. They have an easy, though high-stepping, gait suitable for a smooth carriage ride. Hackney horses and ponies are usually solid colored.

Recently I splurged on a carriage ride around Central Park in New York City, just so I could experience the work of a lovely bay Hackney.

Haflinger

Haflingers are most recognizable by their light gold to golden chestnut color, with flaxen mane and tail. Their distinctive physical characteristics include a height between 13 and 15 hands, a well-muscled body, and a noble head with large, expressive eyes. They're athletic and well balanced, working easily on steep slopes. Personality traits include high intelligence and a willingness to learn. Haflingers are known to be friendly and to enjoy human company. Most people don't start working Haflingers until the animals are four years old, but they may stay active up to forty years.

A friend of mine farms and raises Haflingers. She does attempt to sell the horses, but her Haflingers are so sweet that she ends up keeping more of them than she puts up for sale.

HANOVERIAN

Hanoverians are large horses, standing about 16 hands high. They are known for their strength and endurance, as well as their grace and beauty. Hanoverian horses may be any solid color. They are extremely athletic and often show up in Olympic equestrian and jumping competitions.

When I was eight, I begged to go to a horse camp and learn to jump the camp's Hanoverian mares. My life's savings got me only one lesson, but to this day I remember the experience of sailing over a hurdle on that amazing horse. Hanoverians are terrific show jumpers and great dressage horses.

LIPIZZANER

Lipizzaners are the famous white horses of the Spanish Riding School of Vienna, Austria. Champions in dressage and classic equitation, they are known to be intelligent, willing, and born performers, among the best athletes in the world. The horses are compact and muscled, yielding a controlled, compressed power. They're born dark, but their coats get lighter as they grow older, turning pure white by age ten. Traditionally, only the stallions are ridden and schooled. They can be recognized by their grace and thick, beautifully arched necks, powerful legs, sturdy bodies, small ears, and dark eyes.

If you've never seen Lipizzaners perform, you need to. If you can't make it to a live performance, there are DVDs that show their amazing performance, and you can get an idea of what Lipizzaners are all about.

MALAPOLSKI

Malapolski is a Polish breed of light draft horse. These farm horses are strong and versatile. They stand between 15.2 and 16.2 hands high and are usually solid, dark colors.

I lived in Poland for a while after I got out of college, when Poland was still an Iron Curtain country controlled by communist Russia. There were two kinds of farms: independent farms, plowed by horses; and communist communal farms that could afford tractors. Horse-plowed fields outproduced the tractor-driven fields at better than three to one.

MISSOURI FOX TROTTER

This breed of pleasure horse originated in the Ozarks and rural parts of Missouri. The breed is characterized by a unique four-beat gait, valued for its natural smoothness. In this sure-footed gait, the horse prances out in front, while trotting with the hind legs.

Where I grew up in northwest Missouri, there weren't many Missouri Fox Trotters. But when I did see one, I longed to sit in the saddle for that smooth, rocking-chair gait.

MORGAN

The Morgan horse was the first American breed, developed in colonial New England from a stallion owned by Justin Morgan. The breed is characterized by muscular hindquarters, dished face, and sturdy build. Most Morgans

range from 14.2 to 15.2 hands and are dark and solid colored, with a few white markings. They are known to be good-natured and willing, ideal family horses.

Misty, my black gelding and best friend growing up, was a Morgan (not registered). His nature couldn't have been sweeter. Like other Morgans, Misty was at ease under Western or English tack. He was the all-American, all around horse.

MUSTANG

Mustangs are descended from horses that escaped when they were brought into Mexico by Spaniards in the sixteenth century. The horses were recaptured by Native Americans and soon spread throughout the West. Technically, that makes mustangs *feral*, rather than wild, because they descend from horses that were once domesticated.

Today, descendants of the first mustangs, protected by federal laws and adoption programs, still roam parts of the American West. Mustangs come in a variety of colors and shapes, from beautiful, sturdy horses to scrawny broomtails that aren't so attractive.

I would love to watch mustangs in the wild, but I've only seen them in rescues. I "owned" one for a year, through giving to a mustang rescue. I donated

PONIES OF CHINCOTEAGUE

Ponies on the islands of Chincoteague and Assateague, off the Eastern coast of the United States, are some of the last wild horses in the world.

a certain amount of money to aid mustangs. In return, the agency sent me a photo of a mustang that was designated as mine for one year. It was a great way for them to raise money. You can help support the remaining herds of mustangs by becoming involved with horse rescues, like the Wild Horse Sanctuary, Wild Horse Foundation, and the Bureau of Land Management's Wild Horse and Burro Program.

PAINT AND PINTO

Both paints and pintos have predominantly two-colored coats, spotted or splashed. But a paint horse must also be purebred quarter horse or registered Thoroughbred stock. Pintos can be any breed, as long as they have the right spotted markings. Paints are generally stocky, like quarter

horses, with short backs and quick speed. They're known to be easygoing and good-natured.

Cheyenne is sorrel-and-white spotted, a paint with quarter horse blood. My first horse, Sugar, was a pinto, a mystery breed, but lovely brown and white spots. There are two main types of coloring for the spotted horse: ovaro, a solid darker coat with large splashes of white; and tobiano, a white coat with large splashes of solid color. A third type of color pattern is a combination of these two: tovero. Characteristics include dark coloring around the ears, chest spots, flank spots, and dark coloring at the base of the tail. One or both eyes will be blue.

PASO FINO

Paso Fino is an old breed, developed by Spanish landowners. Pasos have a natural lateral gait that gives a comfortable ride. They are characterized by great endurance and toughness. They may be small and graceful or large and powerful.

When I traveled in Mexico, I rented a Paso Fino so that I could gallop on the beach. Although I'm not sure the horse was a registered Paso Fino—no smooth gait or delicate step—she let me ride her into the ocean, so that was good enough for me.

SHETLAND PONY

Shetlands are a breed of small horse, measuring under 10.2 hands, or 11.2 for American Shetlands. They are tough and strong for their size, with short legs and thick coats. They're known to be intelligent and fairly gentle, although they can show a stubborn streak.

My first 4-H leader owned Shetlands and let horseless 4-H kids ride them sometimes. Often, the experience was enough to convince the rider to consider a different breed. Shetlands can be affectionate and wonderful child ponies. But if they're not trained properly, they can be ornery, headstrong little guys.

STANDARDBRED

A breed of harness racers, Standardbreds got their name from the practice of requiring the horses to meet a timed trotting standard, a mile in two and a half minutes. Standardbreds are developed as trotters or pacers and usually reach 15 or 16 hands. They are dark colored, tough, and calm natured.

Our Amish neighbors in Ohio often buy Standardbreds from horse traders who pick up ex–harness racers. These trotters are ideal buggy horses. Hickory, their current trotter, can trot fast without breaking into a canter that might tear up a buggy.

TENNESSEE WALKING HORSE

The walking horse descends from Thoroughbreds, Standardbreds, Morgans, Saddlebreds, and Pacers. But the breed has a distinguishing conformation. Walkers are compact and powerful, with high tails, short backs, and sloping hindquarters. They move in graceful, smooth, and refined gaits that include the running walk characteristic of the breed.

It's easy to pick out a Tennessee walking horse at a show. They're the horses with the no-bounce gaits: a flat walk, a running walk, and a high, smooth canter that rocks. The running walk has four beats, with head nodding in time and teeth clicking the whole way.

THOROUGHBRED

Thoroughbreds stand 15 to 17 hands tall, with a lean and athletic build, deep chest, and refined head. They may be any solid color, and some may have markings on the legs and face. They're famous for stamina and heart, racing at tracks around the world. Thoroughbreds tend to be high-strung.

Although I've watched Thoroughbreds race, and I loved seeing those sleek, fast horses run, I admit I didn't totally enjoy the experience. The horses seemed so high-strung and nervous that they made me nervous too.

TRAKEHNER

Standing 16 to 17 hands high, Trakehners are among the lightest and most refined horses in the world. Although now they're generally seen in horse shows and ridden as pleasure horses, they used to be valued cavalry mounts.

A horse friend of mine runs an indoor and outdoor boarding and training camp. She uses Trakehners to teach show jumping and dressage because hers are eager to please, intelligent, and accepting . . . not to mention the fact that they're gorgeous.

So many horses, so little time.

THE BEST-LOOKING HORSE

In the end, what breed is best? What really makes a great horse?

Out of all the horses my sister and I grew up with, I'd have to say that Rocket (buckskin) and Sugar (pinto) probably had the worst conformation, or physical build. Neither one had registration papers. In retrospect, Rocket was probably a tad swaybacked, and pictures of Sugar make her look pretty plain. Still, those were the perfect horses for us. We grew up with them and learned from them. They were kind and patient teachers.

Unfortunately, the same can't be said of Seabreeze, our five-gaited American Saddlebred. Lovely breed, perfect conformation, but imperfect disposition.

The best horse for you is the one who will become your best friend.

~ PART FIVE ~

FRIENDSHIP
FROM THE GROUND UP

16

Good Ground Manners

We've already talked a good deal about relating to horses on the ground. Before we zero in on building good ground manners in horses, we need to make sure we've got good ground manners ourselves.

Good People Manners

- Safety first! Hang with horses who like people. Listen to people who know how to handle horses. Follow every rule in the stable, and add some good rules yourself. Horses are bigger than you are. Pay attention!
- Be calm and peaceful around horses. No sudden movements.
- Be dependable and trustworthy by being consistent in care.
- Stay out of the blind spots. Stand to the side in plain view.
- If you can, work from the left side. Most horses are trained from the left side. Don't assume that something learned on the left has also been

learned on the right. Horses process information differently, with "two brains" that don't always communicate well with each other.

- Don't stand behind your horse when you groom her. You can pull her tail to one side to brush it.
- Be patient. Give your horse time to respond, or greet you, or get past fears.
- Wear boots. Thick boots. You *will* get your foot stepped on eventually. Never wear sandals or tennis shoes!
- Don't wrap lead ropes, reins, or lunge lines around your hand—ever. Any horse can get scared and take off.
- Don't visit your horse just to ride. Hang out.
- Enjoy your horse! Play, laugh, love.

R-E-S-P-E-C-T

Good manners are based on mutual respect. When you were young and your parents insisted you say "please" and "thank you," or asked you to excuse yourself from the table, or told you not to interrupt, the rules of being polite probably seemed boring. So did opening the door for someone or letting someone else go in ahead of you. But hopefully, showing respect forged some solid relationships, especially if you were shown respect in return.

It works the same way with your horse. You shouldn't startle your horse, and she shouldn't startle you. You shouldn't crowd her, and she shouldn't crowd you. Neither of you should be obnoxious or disrespectful.

If you ask a horse to do something, he should try to do it. But you should have the patience to help him understand the request and know how to respond. And don't forget to thank him when he does. Good manners will cement a good relationship.

This book isn't intended as a manual or how-to on the art of training horses on the ground. But a few tips from *You and Your Horse* might help keep your ground relationship in good condition. And be sure to check out the list of safety links and sources at the end of the book.

Stable Manners

All of us want our friends to be glad to see us, right? In time, your horse will recognize your smell and maybe even give you that wonderful greeting, the nicker. But at the very least, your horse should not be rude.

When you come into your horse's stall, he needs to face you. You can't accept having him turn his hind end toward you. It's rude, and it's unsafe. You can shake a little oats in a bucket or show up with an apple. But you can't do that all the time. If your horse refuses to face you, even for a handout, you may need to ask for help in educating him.

Your horse shouldn't crowd you in the stall or anywhere else. That's rude. But if you try to move him away by pushing him, or forcing him over, you lose. Every time. Instead of trying to be the forceful "big brother," you can try being the pesky "little brother." You can't force your horse, but you can annoy him if you're patient and persistent. If Cheyenne doesn't feel like moving over when I ask her to, if I want to brush the side closest to the stall, I ask again. And again. And again. All I do is press my finger to her shoulder. Then I let it up. Then I press it again, then release. It doesn't take long for her to get so annoyed with me that she'll move out of the way. A safety tip is to be sure your horse is tied while you're in the stall with her.

The same annoying strategy works if Cheyenne decides she wants to rush me when I'm leading her to the barn. That's rude. But I'm simply not strong enough to hold her back with the lead rope or to block her from the front. I wouldn't want to do that anyway—it would be rude on my part. Instead I settle for being annoying, a role I've come to enjoy. If Cheyenne tries to get ahead of me when I'm leading, I make her circle, leading her in a tight circle to the left. If she tries to get ahead again, I'll circle again. When we first got her, I'd have to circle a dozen times before she gave up. Now it only takes once, or not at all. Here's another safety tip: The safest way to lead your horse is with a lead rope. If you try to lead with the halter only, your fingers could get caught in the halter.

Your horse may need you to be annoying in different ways. You'll be able to adjust your behavior and learn the best way to handle your horse if you pay close attention to his reactions. Moby didn't care when I made her turn in circles. She just didn't seem to get annoyed at that one. But she hated to be backed up. So of course that's what I did whenever she tried to push me. With no force or anger or frustration on my part, I'd simply stop, turn around, and have her back up.

REWARD GOOD MANNERS

Reward good manners, and don't reward bad manners. That sounds obvious, but you may not always realize that you're rewarding your horse. And if you don't realize it, your horse may get the wrong idea.

For example, our horse Butch drove us crazy by backing when we wanted to go forward. So what did we do when he pulled his backing-up stunt and backed a hundred yards? We'd get off his back and go ride one of the other horses. We rewarded our backward horse for doing the wrong thing! We didn't mean to, but we did. No wonder he did it so often.

Seabreeze was the least friendly horse we ever owned, a high-strung, five-gaited American Saddlebred, which we kept for less than a year. She had the nasty and dangerous habit of rearing whenever the slightest thing upset her. When she reared, my sister got off as fast as she could and called it a day. And that was Seabreeze's reward for rearing. She got left alone.

Rocket, our buckskin, surprised us by being able to leap over the makeshift jumps we set up in the pasture. Whenever she felt like it, she could sail over anything we put up. But she tired of jumping fast, and I was convinced that she started knocking down our pole jumps on purpose. The fun was out of the game for us, too. So we stopped. That was her reward. She was being rewarded for doing the wrong thing. If we'd realized what we were doing, we could have used that same reward for good behavior and stopped when she was still clearing the jumps.

If your horse loves being scratched, then scratching can be a great reward. When she picks up her hoof for you, scratch her. Cheyenne loves being scratched on the withers. When I'm riding and want to reward her for cantering on cue in the right lead, I scratch her withers.

Rewards can come in many shapes and forms for a horse. A handful of oats, a carrot, or a watermelon rind can serve as a great reward. But there are hundreds of non-food rewards too. Sometimes leaving your horse alone is a reward. When you stop annoying him (pressing his shoulder or turning him in a circle), that's a reward. Letting him do something he wants to do—heading back to the barn, slowing to a walk, speeding to a gallop, running free in the pasture—that's a reward. Fussing over him when he does something right—that's a reward.

Punishing bad manners can backfire on you. One of my horse friends growing up used to get so angry at her pony for running away from her in the pasture that she'd take her frustrations out on the pony once she did catch him. She'd smack him or jerk the lead rope to punish him for running from her. But the logical horse interpretation would be that the punishment came because he'd allowed himself to get caught. He didn't get smacked when he was running from her. He got smacked when she caught him.

Turning-Out Manners

When you turn out your horse to the pasture, it's natural for him to feel like kicking up his heels or racing through the pasture, giddy with freedom. But if he does this before you're safely out of the way, then that's bad manners.

Be careful turning out your horse. It's easy to get kicked, run over, bumped, or worse. Ever watch horses race through a gate at the same time? It's not a pretty sight. Lead your horse all the way into the pasture. Then you can turn him around so he's facing you and the gate. Turn him loose and step backward through the gate, keeping your eye on him.

A Grounded Friendship

Ground manners are important in your relationship with your horse. You should be spending much more time on the ground with your horse than you do riding. If the only time you met up with your friend was when you wanted something, you'd probably never develop a rewarding friendship (and your friend might stop answering your calls). Horses feel the same way. They'd love to be your friend and hang out with you, not just when you're riding, but when you're on the ground.

You can't expect your horse to have good manners when you're in the saddle if she's rude when you're on the ground.

17

GOOD GROOMING

HOW HORSES GROOM EACH OTHER

Watch a group of horses in the pasture, or even two horses together. One of the main ways horses show affection is through mutual grooming. You can learn a lot by observing a grooming session.

My Misty was a strong alpha horse, a leader, who kept Rocket, my sister's buckskin, in line. Because Misty dominated Rocket, taking her leftover grain, bossing her to a different part of the pasture, I was never certain that the two horses were best friends . . . until I watched them in a mutual grooming session. Rocket usually started it, and Misty almost always ended it. But I could tell that the grooming itself was loved by both horses.

First they'd sniff each other. Then they'd sidle closer and face opposite directions, until Rocket could reach Misty's mane. For a while, it looked like they'd agreed to nibble manes. But from there, the nibbling moved to the sides of the neck, the shoulder, down the back, and all the way to the base of the tail. They nibbled and teeth-scratched each other in those hard-to-reach places.

Once, I saw them swap sides and do the same grooming routine on the other side.

The dynamics changed when we pastured three horses together. But on hot summer afternoons, I might catch all three horses huddled under a tree, ganging up on the flies, swishing tails in a mutual fly-swatting routine.

YOUR TURN TO GROOM

There are thick books on how to groom a horse, how to bathe, brush, massage, and shine that coat until it's show-worthy. It's great to learn all you can about caring for your horse.

But there's more to grooming than making your horse look fancy. Here are some ideas you can try, things that might please your horse and build that friendship.

- Read your horse's reaction to everything you do. Misty loved it when I brushed his black coat the wrong way before smoothing it down again. But Towaco hated that. I could tell the first day I

WHAT FEELS GOOD?

Learn what your horse likes. One mare may hate having her ears scratched, but another might love it. You may enjoy stroking your horse's muzzle, but it's no good if *she* doesn't like it.

Don't you love it when your auntie pinches your cheeks to show how much she loves you? Probably not. Make sure you're not the cheek-pinching aunt to your horse.

got him. His skin tightened and twitched, and I knew he wasn't enjoying the same grooming Misty had. Pay attention.

- Use grooming time as a bonding time. Always groom your horse before you exercise her or ride her. But don't just groom to ride. Bring her in for a massage, a nice, soft brushing. It's prime hanging-out time with your horse.

- Don't over-wash your horse. Washing removes the natural oils that will repel water.

- Keep a hand on your horse, following each brushstroke with a stroke of your hand.

- Be sure to keep contact with your horse as you move around his back or into his blind spots. Talk to him, so he knows where you are at all times.

- Remember that horses itch where they can't scratch. When you're grooming, get those hard-to-reach spots. Be a great grooming partner, and your horse will look forward to your visits.

- Don't use the curry (the hard rubber brush) on a horse's face, flank, legs, or bone. That hurts. Just keep brushing and brushing the legs. Don't use your big brush on the face. There are face brushes or dry sponges. But you can also use your fingernails, which most horses love.

- If you brush with a flick of the wrist, you get out dust that's next to the skin.

- A stable towel is a great tool and good for finishing the grooming process.

HOOVES

Is there anything more important to a horse's well-being than his hooves? All that weight rests on four small hooves that trek through mud, dirt, and muck. A good place to begin grooming is at the hoof.

- Before you lift that hoof, take your time and run your hand down your horse's leg.
- Use a good hoof pick, still the cheapest thing you'll buy for your horse and the most essential. Begin at the heel and move forward. Clean the grooves of the *frog*, the soft V on the underside of the hoof. Use the hoof pick to reach debris under the shoe.
- You have to be the one who decides when the

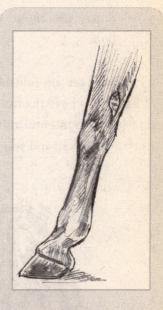

WHAT ARE CHESTNUTS?

Chestnuts are the dried-looking, horny, scablike things on the inside of all four legs. A chestnut is the remnant of a toe, something the earliest horses had. No two chestnuts are alike, just like fingerprints.

hoof goes back down. Set it down slowly and gently, before your horse can rip it out of your hands.

- Safety tip: Never kneel or sit to clean out a hoof.

Finally, let 'em roll! I know we want a clean horse, and it's tough to have the horse you just spent an hour grooming turn around and roll in the nearest muddy spot. But they love to roll, and you have to let them.

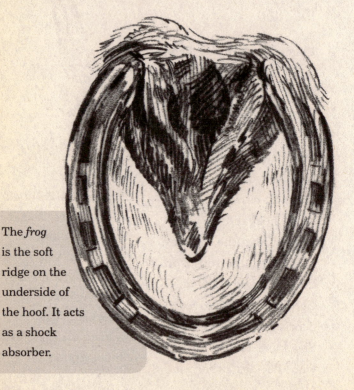

The *frog* is the soft ridge on the underside of the hoof. It acts as a shock absorber.

18

How to (and Not to) Catch a Horse

Almost every rider has experienced the frustration of not being able to catch her horse. Rocket could make complete idiots out of my sister and me as we chased her around the pasture until she finally allowed us to catch her.

Remember Horse Nature

When you think about catching your horse, keep in mind your horse's nature.

- Horses are prey. Their instincts tell them they have two choices when someone comes running at them: fight or flight. They don't like fighting, so they take off.
- Your horse isn't in a hurry. If you are, then you're bound to be in for a struggle. Instead, yawn and sigh as you enjoy the day and move closer.
- Don't assume your horse recognizes you. Horses don't seem to see in detail, although they can see movement far away. You could be

a mountain lion. And if you're wearing some-thing flappy, like a coat, then who knows what you could be?

- What makes you look like a predator? Preda-tors sneak up on their prey. So keep in mind your horse's blind spots, and stay out of them. Don't walk straight up to your horse, and don't approach from behind. Signal your entry into the pasture. Whistle, sing, call.

- Don't face off squarely. Your horse sees that action as aggressive, challenging.

- Hey, admit it: Who wouldn't rather hang out-side and eat all day than let somebody sit on his back and boss him around? It's logical that a horse might play hard to get. Don't get angry or frustrated. If you're calm, your horse will be too. Expect to catch your horse. In fact, don't think of it as "catching." That implies grasping and grabbing, which you never want to do.

Playing Hard to Get

If your horse is playing hard to get, so should you. (My older sister always claimed this strategy works with guys.) Don't just walk straight up to your horse. Instead, act as if you're going for one of the other horses in the pasture. Did you ever try to get one horse out of a herd of horses? That will be the one who walks away from you, while the others keep grazing. So act as if you really want a different horse, then angle over to yours. Keep glancing at the other horses and look at the ground as you walk right up to yours.

Make coming in to you worth it to your horse. He should expect some loving, grooming, and/or food when he comes to your call. If you call him in only for a shot or a vet exam, he may not trust your call.

As you get more used to your horse, and he accepts you as the lead in this relationship, he should follow you, even without a halter and lead rope. Watch the way horses follow one another, and imitate them. Eye contact plays an important role in the cues you give your horse. Glancing directly into his eyes can serve as a warning that he's walking too close or that you might not accept his following you right now. Then drop your gaze immediately, dropping your shoulder slightly and curving a step away from him. He should follow you, or at least move his head toward you, an action you can reward.

HORSE GENTLING

If you've watched modern horse gentlers, or read their books, you've probably heard about round pens and the technique called joining up developed by Monty Roberts, the "Horse Whisperer." Monty Roberts and others changed the way many horse trainers work with horses. People like Roberts, Pat Parelli, John Lyons, Robert Lyons, Cherry Hill, Linda Tellington-Jones, and others encourage people to educate horses by learning to communicate with them. They rely on nonverbal horse language, body language horses use with one another.

I can't begin to explain all the theories of horse gentling. But I'll give you an overview of how it works.

Round Pens

A round pen is just that, a small pen to help you train your horse in a more controlled environment. The pen lets you keep your horse close enough that you can read each other's body language.

Since a horse will run away in a bigger space, that natural instinct is curbed in the round pen. A frightened or nervous horse can run, but he won't get anywhere. He'll still be close enough to you for you to help. Because you don't have to worry about him running away, you can let him have time to think and run and think and run. Being able to run lets him stay calm enough to think.

Partnering with Your Horse

The goal of the process is to develop a partnership with your horse, in which you're the leader but also a partner. You should read Monty Roberts's books, or watch his videos, or ask for help from someone who's used the joining-up methods. But the basic idea is to get your horse to submit to the pecking order, to get him to stop and turn toward you, ready to be caught by you.

A horse is started running in a circle, lapping the round pen. When you think you have his attention, step back. Then look for his reaction. If he stops, step back again and see if he turns his head to you. If he does, take another step away from his head, but move toward his flank. What you want is for him to face you. If he does that, you're in. You've done it. Catch him, scratch him. Tell him he's amazing. Then release him as his reward.

Chances are, though, it won't be so easy. If he doesn't stop, or if he walks off without looking at you, then you make him run his circles again. And you start the whole process over. And over. And over.

What I like about this method is the way it imitates horse language in order to cement a horse-human friendship. Monty Roberts spent years developing his techniques, so don't expect to pull it off in a day. Begin by studying and learning "horse" before you try to speak "horse." Observe horses. And of course, safety first!

Use only those tips and practices that work for you and your horse. Remember that your goal is to have the best relationship you can with horses, to get horses to love you as much as you love them.

Then, when you and your horse have a good relationship, based on mutual respect and good ground manners, it's time to talk about riding.

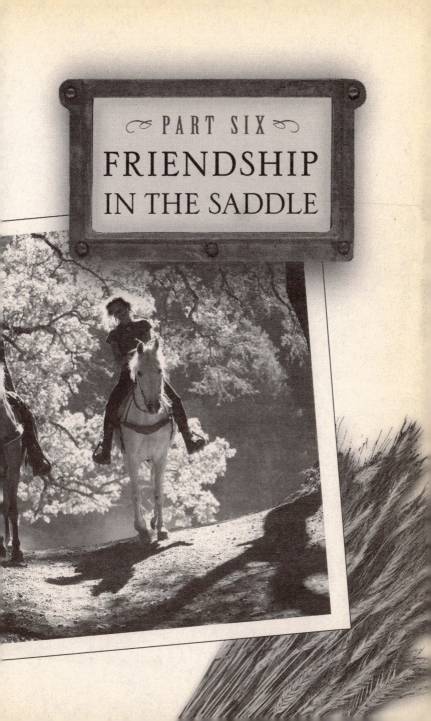

PART SIX

FRIENDSHIP
IN THE SADDLE

19

The Rider's Attitude

It's amazing that a thousand-plus-pound animal will allow someone one-tenth his size to sit on his back and choose where they'll both go and at what pace.

But horses do. And if respect and friendship have been established between rider and horse, the ride should be a wonderful experience.

This isn't a how-to-ride book. I'm not even sure you can learn to ride by reading about it, although learning about horses and riding will help you improve your riding skills. My goal isn't to replace hands-on instruction or horseback riding lessons. The safest way to learn to ride is from an experienced teacher on a trustworthy horse. An instructor can help you develop safe riding skills that you'll use for the rest of your riding life.

All I want to do is offer some tips that might help you further your relationship with the horse once you're in the saddle.

Check your Attitude

Nothing is more important than having the right attitude when you ride.

- *Be safe.* Do everything you can to make sure you're safe.
- *Helmet.* Be sure you're wearing a riding helmet approved by the American Society of Testing Materials (ASTM). Check out some of the safety resources at the end of this book.
- *Boots.* Always wear boots when you're riding. The heel helps keep your foot from sliding through the stirrup.
- *Equipment.* Check your tack to make sure it's in good condition. Consider other safe choices in equipment, from safety breakaway stirrups to safety vests.
- *Location.* Choose safe trails and areas for your rides. Ride with a partner when you can.
- *Think like your horse.* Remember what it's like to be a prey animal, on the lookout for predators, ready to run away if necessary.
- *Ride in control.* Don't ride faster than you can control. Know that you can stop your horse easily if you need to.
- *Be understanding.* Your horse may not know voice cues. She may misread your pressure cues. It might take her dozens of repetitions before she "gets" it. She's probably not trying to aggravate you.
- *Be patient.* Your horse might need to check out

that ditch before she'll feel comfortable crossing it. Give her time.

- *Be respectful.* When you ride, show respect to your horse and to other riders. Don't crowd or excite their horses.
- *Relax.* Your horse will pick up your tension and give it right back to you.
- *Be firm and consistent.* You're the alpha. Don't let your horse get away with anything.

TWO TYPES OF
FRIENDLY BRIDLES

A *hackamore* is a style of Western bridle with no bit. It consists of a headstall; the bosal, soft, braided leather that rests on the muzzle; and mecate, or long rein with lead rope.

A *snaffle* is a jointed bit with reins attached to an O-ring or D-ring. It's the mildest bit, and it should be all you'll ever need.

- *Be a partner.* Remember that even though you're the leader, you're also a partner. You and your horse are in this together. Don't draw a line in the sand and make your horse go by that scary barrel no matter how terrified she is. Avoid conflict and silly wars based on pride.

- *Be the rider your horse deserves.* Be the one he'll look for and turn to for answers, protection, and support.

- *Have fun!* Enjoy the ride. So what if your heels aren't down far enough or the angle of your shoulders is off. You can work on the fine points. Your primary goal should be to have a great ride, great for you and great for the horse—and safe for both of you.

STAYING IN TUNE

All of your senses should be in play when you're riding.

- Keep watch. Look up and past your horse's ears.

- I like to look where I want to go. There's a saying about jumping horses that says the rider needs to send her heart over the fence first, and the horse will follow.

- Your vision is limited when you're on a horse. You can see the crest of the neck, the withers, parts of the jaw, the poll, that soft area between the ears. So pay attention to your horse's ears. They'll give you clues to what your horse is paying attention to.

- Feel your horse. Even through a saddle, you can feel a horse tensing his back muscles, gathering himself, arching his spine, getting ready to buck.

- Eventually you'll be able to feel your horse's rhythm in every gait and go with it.

ANTICIPATE

- When horses are frightened, they shy. They dance sidewise, or bolt sideways, or put on the brakes fast. Even a horse that's been *sacked out*, rubbed all over with a crackly sack to desensitize him, will shy if he's really scared. Be on the lookout for the signs your horse will give you *before* he shies.

- Before a horse shies, her ears will prick forward to get in more information. She might lift her head and snort. You should be able to feel the tension in her back and see or feel it in her neck. That's your cue to be on the alert. You could turn her and avoid the problem. Or, if you have to continue in the "scary" direction, start talking her out of being scared. Scratch her withers and stay relaxed yourself. Breathe. Laugh.

- If your horse is still too frightened to go on, and you must go on, dismount. Be patient. Show him things aren't so scary after all. Let him see you deal with the situation—walk across the bridge first, handle the object that scares him. Then patiently lead him past the fear, taking one step and giving him as much time as he needs.

- If there's a loud noise behind you, prepare for a quick stop and swift turn toward the noise. Give your horse time to process the information and decide if she's worried about it. If she is, be a good partner and go with her to investigate. Let her see for herself that there's nothing to worry about.

- If you're riding, say, on a trail ride, and your horse's ears go flat back and his tail swishes fast, he's getting angry about something behind him. Another horse may be crowding into his space. Move ahead if you can. Or politely ask the guy behind you to back off a bit.

- If your horse stretches her neck and ducks her head, with her ears forward, she's probably about to take off on you, or at least speed up. Shift your weight back, pull back lightly. Release. Pull back lightly again, if you must. Or simply change directions, pulling your horse off her planned course.

- Changing a horse's direction can solve a multitude of problems and would-be problems in the saddle. You can't win a tug-of-war with your horse, but you can almost always get your way, eventually, by pulling one rein until he turns.

20

AVOID CONFLICT

True, you are the alpha. Your horse should look to you for leadership and try to please you and do what you want him to. But why not return the favor? Whenever possible, whenever it doesn't honestly take something away from your horse, look for the end run around conflict. I'm sure there will be trainers who disagree with me, by the way. But by getting my horse and myself out of conflicts, I think I've deepened our friendship and trust.

- If your horse doesn't want to cross that shaky wooden bridge, do you really have to cross it? Isn't there another route? It may take more time, but you'll enjoy the ride.
- If you find yourself fighting to keep your horse in a slow walk or jog because he wants to speed things up, instead of constantly battling the bit, stop. Back him up a good distance. Then go forward. If he tries to speed up again, back up again. Most horses (with the notable exception of Butch the Backing Horse) don't enjoy backing.

Pretty soon your horse will stop fighting you.

- If you can't get your horse to go past something in the pasture, such as a big bale of hay, enlist the help of another horse and rider. Follow them past it. Old Moby served as a reliable guide for Cheyenne on rides into the pasture. Cheyenne was afraid of anything new, but she trusted Moby enough to follow the old mare anyway.

- If your horse takes off and runs away, don't panic. Breathe. Chances are you won't be able to stop him by pulling on the reins. But you can slow him by pulling on one rein and making him turn. He can't run fast in a tight circle, and he'll eventually stop.

- Cheyenne hated standing in the cross-ties for grooming or saddling. When we first got her and I naively stood her in the cross-ties, she immediately reared. And reared. Then she backed up until both leads snapped right out of the wood rafters. I tried to get her used to the ties. But even when she stood still for me, her body was too tense to enjoy grooming. So I tried grooming her in her stall. Now I saddle her in her stall too. And sometimes I groom her out in the pasture, with no lead at all. She enjoys it too much to walk off on me.

- I'd love to tell you that you'll never fall off your horse if you follow all the tips, but it's not true.

Most horse riders take a fall now and again. If you fall, get your feet out of the stirrups. When you hit the ground, roll. Roll out of the way. And relax. I've lost count of the number of falls I've taken. I don't recommend falling, but it's usually not so bad. Usually. The one time I fell off Cheyenne was the worst fall of my life. It was my fault. I hadn't ridden in January or February because of the snow. March hit with sunshine, but cold, brisk winds. I couldn't wait. I hopped on without a saddle, and she bucked me off. What was I thinking?

- You can head off many falls before they come. First, make sure you're protected with a helmet and boots, long-sleeved shirts and long pants or jeans, and a safety vest, if warranted. Pay attention to your horse. If he's worried about something, don't simply keep going. Deal with it. You can usually sense a buck early by feeling the tension in your horse's back. He'll try to put his head down because he needs it down if he wants to get his hind end up. Foil his plan. Don't let him get his head down. Keep pulling up on the reins.

Unfortunately, bad things happen to good horses and good riders. Whenever you can, look for ways to avoid conflict.

21

Tips on Techniques

Whether you ride English or Western, dressage or jumping, certain commonsense tips could help make your riding experience better for you and for your horse.

- Relax. Breathe. Don't worry so much about the angle of your shoulders and position of your legs that you forget to have a good time riding.
- Sit naturally—not stiff and straight, not slouched over.
- Think about what you want your horse to do. Your horse is so sensitive that she can feel a fly on her back. Think she feels you there? Yes! She may feel what you want before you ask her to do it. If you want to go forward, think "forward" as you lean slightly forward. You might not even have to lean.
- Ride a balanced seat. You're not balanced if you're flopping all over the place. And don't try to use the bridle for balance either. Instead, sink into your seat, into the saddle, and catch

the rhythm of your horse. You'll know when you have it.

- A good seat ends up with ear, shoulder, hip, and heel aligning. Resist the urge to lean too far forward or too far back.

- If you keep your heels down, it helps you sink deeper into the seat of your horse, where you can find his rhythm.

- But if you try to force the perfect riding position, you can make yourself crazy. It will come if you relax.

- Move with your horse. Go on and exaggerate the motions until you know you have the feel. And if you feel in sync for only two minutes, then be ecstatic over those two minutes. Don't fret about the other fifty-eight minutes. Fun, remember?

- Ask nicely when you want your horse to perform. You can't force a horse.

- Don't jam your feet too far into your stirrups. Feel the stirrup on the balls of your feet, and be ready to take your feet out if you need to.

- Keep your lower legs quiet unless you want something.

- If you lift the reins, it usually signals your horse to get ready to go forward or faster. Be sure you mean it if you lift reins.

- Find out if the horse you're riding neck-reins.

Neck-reining is when you hold both reins in one hand, usually your off hand—left, if you're right-handed—and turn your horse by laying the off rein on his neck. For example, if you're riding Western and want to turn left, with both reins in your left hand, all you have to do is turn over your left hand, moving it slightly left. The right rein touches your horse's neck, neck-reining him to turn left.

In the End, in the Saddle

With so many things to think about when you get on that horse, it's easy to lose sight of what really matters.

It happened to me a couple of years ago, and it was a lesson I don't want to forget. I got a terrific assignment to write an article about horses in Ireland for *Western Horseman*. When I arrived at Drumcoura Equestrian Centre, in County Leitrim, a beautiful horse ranch and stable, I think the stable hands expected me to be Annie Oakley incarnate, straight from the American Wild West. The young women who cared for the horses and gave riding instruction greeted me as if I were Queen of the Cowgirls. I admit that I enjoyed that more than I should have.

The first morning out, the stable hands were waiting for me. They handed over their most spirited horse, set out a racing pattern, and watched, eager to see how a real cowgirl performed in barrel racing. I loved the horse, but I couldn't keep those infernal patterns in my head. I forgot whole segments of the routines. And I could read the disappointment in the Irish horsewomen's faces. I was a failure, not at all what they'd expected.

That night I figured out what had gone wrong. I'd been so eager to please my audience and to make a good impression that I'd forgotten to enjoy the ride.

The next day I asked if we could just go riding.

We set out into the forests and hills of County Leitrim, galloping in open fields, trekking carefully on hillsides and rocky crests. It was pure fun. And I'd almost missed it by caring too much how I looked to other people.

As you train and drill your horse, as you practice and perform, don't forget to simply ride your horse and enjoy the ride.

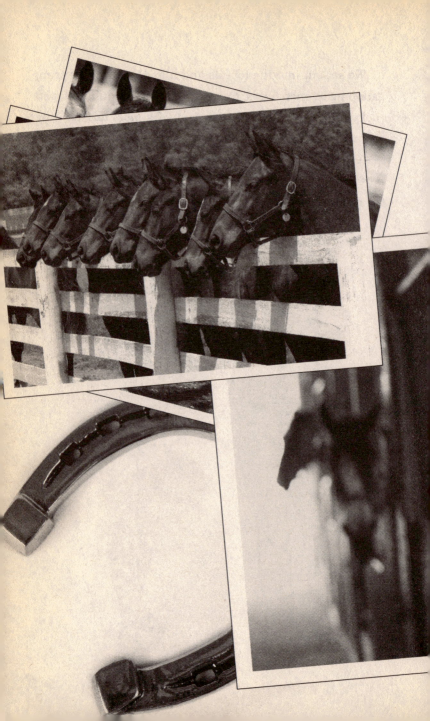

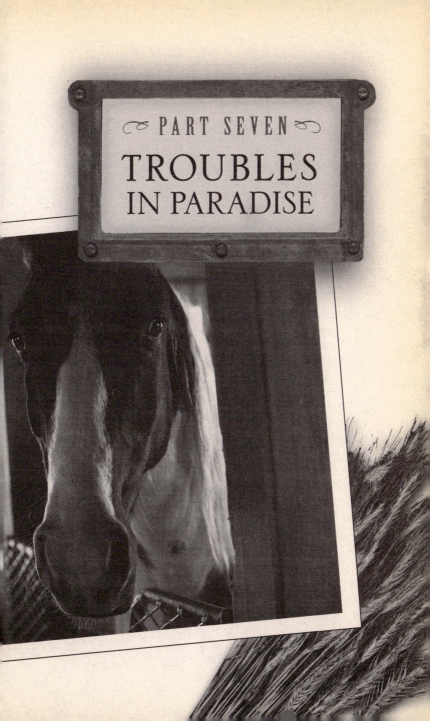

PART SEVEN

TROUBLES
IN PARADISE

22

STABLE VICES

No horse is perfect. Each animal you deal with will probably come with his own set of problems, just like each friend you make at school has his or her own problems to bring to your relationship. Then together you have to develop a few problems of your own to add to the mix.

When it comes to "problem horses," or problems with horses, most of the trouble can be traced back to poor handlers or to boring living conditions.

You won't find magic solutions in this section. But it might help to touch on a few common problems and a couple of tips that have worked for me with some of the horses I've known.

Stable vices are bad behaviors horses play out in stables or barns and stalls. A number of bad habits can develop in a horse that's been cooped up in a stable most of the day. The vices almost always stem from pure boredom. And nearly every problem can be helped by giving the horse more pasture time.

- *Pawing, kicking the door, bumping walls.* You'd

probably feel like doing the same thing if you were cooped up in that stall. Keep in mind how curious horses are and how much they enjoy the company of others.

- *Cribbing.* Cribbing is the nasty habit of chewing on things, like the stall door, the fence, or trees. In many stables you can see doors with an unnatural dip in the middle, where horses have gnawed. Horses have a tough enough time digesting food. Wood is a bad thing to put into their stomachs.

- *Wind-sucking.* When the horse who chews wood, or cribs, holds the wood in his teeth, then inhales, sucking in air to his stomach, it's called wind-sucking. And it's a very dangerous habit.

- *Weaving.* If a horse gets bored enough in that stall, she may rock back and forth, from one leg to the other, weaving her head.

- *Box walking.* A horse can get so bored that he'll pace in his stall, straining ligaments with constant turns.

The obvious solution to stable vices is to turn out the horse. Give him more pasture time. Horses naturally graze twelve to sixteen hours a day, play with other horses, walk around, keep an eye on the world around them. Being cooped up goes against their nature.

But if you can't turn out the horse for longer periods of

time, you can try to make that stall as interesting as possible. There are stall toys, which some claim can help with boredom. You can feed your horse more often, in smaller portions. Hay nets hung from the ceiling can make eating more interesting and last longer. Some horses like big rubber balls. Others might go for a gunnysack filled with cans. Or you could get him a companion—a horse, dog, cat, goat.

TOP PETS (COMPANIONS)
FOR HORSES

- another horse
(always the best
choice, if possible)
- goat
- sheep
- dog
- cat
- chicken

23

PERSONAL PROBLEMS

Through trial and error, my horse friends and I have struggled through a few common problems and stumbled onto solutions that worked for us. Maybe some of these ideas will help you with your "personal" horse problems.

BITING

Angel was a biter from the time he was a foal. Foals inspect things with their mouths—and that includes humans. But biting is a habit that should be stopped early on. I got Angel to stop biting by gently poking my finger into the soft side of his muzzle and saying, "Quit." Angel was one horse I knew I could never let eat out of my hand. My friend Pam couldn't get her older horse to stop biting her until she sprayed his mouth with her pocket-sized breath freshener at the exact moment he bit her.

ANGRY HORSE

Another friend, Debbie, had a beautiful but angry American Saddlebred. I figured the solution would be to find out what made Belle so angry. We finally decided that

Belle was tired of the same dull routine, riding in Debbie's home arena, practicing for horse shows day in and day out. Debbie started riding Belle in the pasture and on dirt roads around the farm, and the horse's mood improved greatly.

UNHAPPY HORSE

Another friend bought a colt and did a great job training him, but the colt always seemed unhappy and lonely to me. Our own foal, Angel, grew up with two mares and no other foals around. If you watch foals play together, you can see the pure joy in their romping. They race and rear and buck. Angel would have preferred playing with yearlings, but she had to settle for my sister and me. So we played with her whenever we could.

HEAD-SHY OR BRIDLE-SHY

Moby hated being bridled. I think that in the past someone must have used a curb bit on her tender mouth, a bit much more severe than my snaffle. As soon as Moby spotted the bridle, she'd jerk up her head and try to dodge the bit. She never tried to run away, but she gave us a time bridling her. All I had to do, though, was bring out the jar of molasses, smear a little on the bit, and let her bring her head down herself. Most horses will go for molasses on the bit. Remember that the horse can't see in front of her, so be sure to stand to the side when you bridle her. Face the same way she is. Be careful of the poll, that soft spot between the ears. If you need to, unbuckle the bridle and put the headgear on first. Make the bridling experience as pleasant as possible.

UNFRIENDLY HORSE

I don't think Seabreeze liked or trusted people. If I had that horse again, I'd try to win her over with laughter, talk, music, scratching, brushing, and treats.

WARNING TO THE WISE

Most horses are ready to be your friend if you're relaxed and friendly yourself. If you're patient and take the time to understand where they're coming from, they'll usually come around.

But it's worth a word of caution here to point out that a few horses, especially severely abused horses, can't be won over by the simple advice in this book. We probably did the right thing selling Seabreeze back to her former owner. The horse was a danger, at least to us, where we were in our horse skills and abilities.

Pay attention to warnings from stable managers, horse owners, and trainers. It's not your job to win over a dangerous horse. There are enough wonderful horses out there waiting for your friendship.

24

GOING ALONG FOR THE RIDE

Not long ago I received a long e-mail from a fan who'd read all my horse fiction books. She wanted to tell me that she'd just gotten her first horse about six months earlier.

This girl loved her horse and wanted to be the best partner, trainer, rider, and friend she could be. And so she'd written to me for help. She asked which aids and methods I thought she should try: the clicker method, pressure-release, voice cues, or others. She'd tried Monty Roberts's round pen, join-up method and couldn't get it to work with her new horse. She'd even tried blowing into her horse's nostril, which she'd picked up from my Winnie the Horse Gentler character. That didn't work either. And now she was concerned because her horse didn't answer her warm greeting by blowing back.

I had answers and opinions on the methods she asked about, but I thought I picked up on something much more important behind the words of her e-mail. And I knew I was right when I got to the last line of her message: "Sometimes I'm so afraid that I'm doing the wrong thing, I can't enjoy the ride."

I wrote back and congratulated her on owning her first horse. I commended her for caring so much and for reading up on the training and care of her horse.

Then I advised her to take a deep breath and go enjoy her horse. That's why she got the horse in the first place. She needed to forget everything else and go have fun with her new friend.

A week later I got an e-mail from her. She'd stopped trying to be the perfect horsewoman and started becoming a grateful companion to her new horse. She was totally in love with her horse and enjoying every minute she spent with him. She knew she had a long way to go, and she still wanted to learn all she could. But she had her priorities straight. She and her horse were on their way to becoming best friends.

Those of you who've cared enough to read this far could end up in the same place as this horse owner. Don't let that happen. Don't worry so much about techniques and tricks that you forget why you love horses in the first place. I'll bet you loved horses before you knew anything about them.

There will always be a lot we don't know, and we'll always do some things wrong. Horses are very forgiving, especially when they know they're loved. Listen to horses and learn to connect with them. Enjoy those stable horses as if they're yours. Be a friend to every horse you meet. They'll teach you what you need to know.

If after reading *You and Your Horse*, you come away with

a better understanding of horses, and a few ideas on how you can become better friends with horses, that's all I ask, all I hope for.

Keep on loving horses, and they'll love you back.

FURTHER RESOURCES

ORGANIZATIONS TO PROMOTE SAFETY IN HORSEMANSHIP

American Association for Horsemanship Safety (AAHS)

1-866-485-6800

4125 Fish Creek Road, Estes Park, CO 80517

http://www.horsemanshipsafety.com/contact.html

American Youth Horse Council

1-800-TRY-AYHC

6660 #D-451 Delmonico, Colorado Springs, CO 80919

http://www.ayhc.com

e-mail: info@ayhc.com

Horsemanship Safety Association

608-767-2593

Ted Marthe

5304 Reeve Road, Mazomanie, WI 53560

http://horsesafety.net

e-mail: hoofbeat@midplains.net

National 4-H Council

301-961-2800

7100 Connecticut Avenue, Chevy Chase, MD 20815

http://www.fourhcouncil.edu/

e-mail: info@fourhcouncil.edu

Find 4-H Cooperative Extension offices in your community:

http://www.csrees.usda.gov/Extension/index.html

Equestrian Medical Safety Association

1-866-441-2632

P.O. Box 91883 Albuquerque, NM 87199

http://www.emsaonline.net

Certified Horsemanship Association

1-800-724-1446

4037 Iron Works Parkway, Ste. 180, Lexington, KY 40511

http://www.cha-ahse.org/

e-mail: clandwehr@cha-ahse.org

American Riding Instructors Association (ARIA)

28801 Trenton Court, Bonita Springs, FL 34134

http://www.riding-instructor.com/

e-mail: aria@riding-instructor.com

American Horse Council

202-296-4031

1616 H Street NW, 7th floor, Washington, DC 20006

http://www.horsecouncil.org/

e-mail: schase@horsecouncil.org

Suggested Reading

Ainslie, Tom, and Bonnie Ledbetter. *The Body Language of Horses.*

New York: William Morrow, 1980.

Blake, Henry. *Talking with Horses.*

North Pomfret, VT: Trafalgar Square Publishing, 1975.

Budd, Jackie. *A-Z of Horse Behavior and Training.*

New York: Howell Book House, 2000.

Burnes, Deborah, ed. *Storey's Horse-Lover's Encyclopedia.*

Pownal, VT: Storey Publishing, 2001.

Chapple, Judy. *Your Horse: A Step-by-Step Guide to Horse Ownership.*

Pownal, VT: Storey Communications, Inc., 1984.

Coggins, Jack. *The Horseman's Bible.*

New York: Doubleday, 1968.

Dawson, Jan. *Teaching Safe Horsemanship: A Guide to English and Western Instruction.*

Pownal, VT: Storey Publishing, 1997.

Dines, Lisa. *The American Mustang Guidebook.*

Minocqua, WI: Willow Creek Press, 2001.

Disston, Marry. *Know All About Horses.*

Hollywood, CA: Wilshire Book Company, 1961.

Draper, Judith. *The Book of Horses and Horse Care.*

London, UK: Anness Publishing Limited, 1996.

Dunning, Pam and Lionel. *Riding School.*

London: Quatro Publishing, 1989.

Edwards, Elwyn Hartley. *The Ultimate Horse Book.*

New York: Dorling Kindersley, Inc., 1991.

Edwards, Elwyn Hartley. *Horses.*

New York: Dorling Kindersley, Inc., 1993.

Haas, Jessie. *Safe Horse/Safe Rider.*

  Pownal, VT: Storey Publishing, 1994.

Hill, Cherry. *Becoming an Effective Rider.*

  Pownal, VT: Storey Publishing, 1991.

Hill, Cherry. *Horse Handling & Grooming.*

  Pownal, VT: Storey Publishing, 1997.

Kimball, Cheryl. *The Everything Horse Book.*

  Avon, MA: Adams Media Corp., 2002.

Lyons, John. *Lyons on Horses.*

  New York: Doubleday, 1991.

Lyons, John. *Communicating with Cues: The Rider's Guide to Training and Problem Solving, Part 1.*

  Greenwich, CT: Belvoir Pub., 1998.

Marlewski-Probert, Bonnie. *Debugging Your Horse.*

  Red Bluff, CA: K & B Products, 1996.

McBane, Susan. *Behavior Problems in Horses.*

  Hollywood, CA: Wilshire Book Company, 1987.

McBane, Susan, and Helen Douglas-Cooper. *Horse Facts.*

  New York: Barnes & Noble Books, 1998.

Mettler, John J., Jr., D.V.M. *Horse Sense: A Complete Guide to Horse Selection & Care.*

  Pownal, VT: Storey Publishing, 1989.

Morris, Desmond. *Horsewatching.*

  New York: Crown, 1989.

Peace, Michael, and Lesley Bayley. *Think Like Your Horse.*

  Devon, UK: David & Charles Books, 2002.

Powell, Sam. *Almost a Whisper.*

  Loveland, CO: Alpine Publications, 1999.

Price, Steven D. *The Horseman's Illustrated Dictionary*.

New York: The Lyons Press, 2000.

Prince, Eleanor F., and Gaydell M. Collier. *Basic Training for Horses: English and Western*.

New York: Doubleday, 1989.

Rashid, Mark. *Considering the Horse: Tales of Problems Solved and Lessons Learned*.

Boulder, CO: Johnson Books, 1993.

Roberts, Monty. *The Man Who Listens to Horses*.

Toronto: Random House of Canada, 2002.

Steffen, Randy. *The Revised Horseman's Scrapbook*.

Colorado Springs, CO: Western Horseman Inc., 1986.

Tellington-Jones, Linda. *Getting in Touch: Understand and Influence Your Horse's Personality*.

North Pomfret, VT: Trafalgar Square Publishing, 1995.

Twelveponies, Mary. *There Are No Problem Horses, Only Problem Riders*.

Boston: Houghton Mifflin Company, 1982.

Wanless, Mary. *The Natural Rider*.

North Pomfret, VT: Trafalgar Square Publishing, 1996.

Watson, Mary Gordon. *Horse: The Complete Guide*.

London, UK: Team Media, Ltd., 1999.

Reader's Note:

Many of these great horse books have been updated since my early version listed here. Be sure to check your local library or bookstore to discover many other fine horse books.